DEMAND & SUPPLY SIDES OF TECHNOLOGICAL INJECTIONS

Bahman Fakhraie, Ph.D.

TECONOMICS OF DEMAND AND SUPPLY SIDES OF TECHNOLOGICAL INJECTIONS IN WEALTH OF NATIONS

By

Dr. Bahman Fakhraie

[December 7, 2004]

FERDAT Publishing, Ogden, UT, USA
Published in Untied States of America
Library of Congress 1222724

$189.95
ISBN 978-0-9852958-3-7
59999>
9 780985 295837

DEDICATION

I thank my immediate family for their patience, Mrs. Kay Davis, Miss Lara F. Fakhraie, Mr. Anayat W. Fakhraie. I am grateful to the late Mr. Anayatollah Fakhraie and Mrs. Fatemeh Bigom Fakhraie, Wayne and Laura Davis. I am thankful to all of family for their many ways of being helpful, as only family can.

ABSTRACT

The supply and demand aspect of technological injections and advancement only partly allow for sustainable economic success. When free perfectly competitive markets are pointed at for sustainable economic advancement, often-derailing details are missing out of these complex strategies for global survival.

Ignorance of such details does not enhance global security but endangers it. An expanding global population needs to employ diminishing global resources to meet demands that without education will implode all systems, as the rate of pollution growth far exceed the capacity of detoxification either natural or manufactured, other issues of health and wellbeing complicate realities, these without prioritization of needs, wants, and without appropriate pricing remain problematic.

In this paper, we study that even segmental corrections and technological injections will yield promising result for the economic-welfare of the globe.

TABLE OF CONTENTS

List of Tables

List of Figures

PREFACE

I am grateful to great many people for their helpful hints, comments, and their tested tolerance on, I hope, very rare occasions. Mostly, I am very thankful to my family for their many ways of being helpful, as only family can. I thank my immediate family for their patience, Mrs. Kay Davis Fakhraie, Miss Lara F. Fakhraie, Mr. Anayat W. Fakhraie. They were patient for dad's prolong preoccupation with his research and studies, which started before they were born, and because he lived it. The errors of course are all mine, as I often alter scripts. I enjoy making mistakes, I am reaching outside my comfort zones, and I am trying to learn anew. I also enjoy catching and correcting my mistakes, it shows I am learning some things new, sometime, for the second time, but the growth is dynamic. You will find most of this scientific research, encourages advanced methodic failures that will yield that rare jewel of success or discovery, that is part of scientific methodology as I have defined it, and as it has been thought and cultivated for centuries, millenniums. I hope I show gratitude, if I am corrected in the many mistakes, I make, if I do not show it I am thinking how to show it. I thank all my family members for their many sacrifices and their love.

In addition, I am grateful to the late Mr. Anayatollah Fakhraie and Mrs. Fatemeh Bigom Fakhraie, since without them I would have not been here, and for their loving and care in good memories. They lived in tumultuous years in a developing country, under the fangs and claws of many forces, including Mother Nature. I recall stories of horse riders, gun hands, and town tenders for my grandparent. that mother and close family had to use bird host and shut gun to defend themselves, for being married to a banker, during a quick experiment with democracy in 1950s. My own life in developing and untamed lands with agriculture, hunting, and growing up, and studies has been full of many rainbows, I recall and remember it all with love, grace, and gratitude. I thank Mr. Houshang Fakhraie for his supporting of my education the best he could. I thank Mr. Fridon Fakhraie My brothers, whom helped in the ways they could for so long, I hope their families and my late and living sisters family do well. The Dezfoli and Iranians family, hard workers, scholars, professors, now some of them worldwide, and my American friends and family, beside my immediate family, they have been more than gracious to me. I wish all lives' good turns be better for them.

The Late senator and Mrs. Frank M Browning, and their great living family members, I have met. They good memory is a lasting tribute to their lives. The late Dr. and Mrs. Pollard, and Dr. and Mrs. Call of USU Logan Utah, while they were doing agricultural and development research in Iran. In memoriam all scholars and great, dear people, their great work are appreciated. Their living family members I met have been kind and generous of heart, spirits, and minds. Also Mr. Dick, and Mrs. Florence Ward with Steve and Barbara, they live in Hawaii. I thank all friends and professors globally, and many global opinion leaders, peace advocates, scholars, fine artists, and national treasures, whom I have met.

I thank Dr. Lance Girton, and Dr. Peter W. Philips, the chair of the Economics department at the University of Utah, and professors Stephen Reynolds, James Patrick Gander, and J. Steven Ott. Special thanks to Dr. S. H. Rokni, world-renowned nuclear physics specialist at Stanford University, E. K. Hunt, Korkut Alp Erturk, and David M. Kiefer. I thank Dr. Khosrow Mostofi, then Director of the UOU Middle East Center, Dr. James Kritzeck, Directors of Graduate Studies, Dr. Hussein Fahim, the department of Anthropology, and Mrs. Lucille Seely, Graduate Fellowships, for their support. I thank Dr. Haideh Salehi, Dr. Robert R. Edminster, and Dr.

Lawrence Nabors. In memoriam, I am grateful for the extended conversations and tea, and friendship of the rare gentle scholar, late professor Ernest William Randa. University of Utah President David W. Pershing, and past president Michael K. Young, Social and Behavioral Sciences Dean M. David Rudd, Graduate school Dean White, Economic Department Chair Thomas Neil Maloney, Dr. Bahman Bakhtiari, UOU Middle East Dept. chair. I thank MISS PICKETT, M. KLEIN, and K. Harward, at Graduate school UOU, and Mary R. Guillory and Tracey Anne Farnsworth at Economic Department.

I beg for your indulgence and patience for these elongated eruditions, and self-indulgence in remembrance of friends and associate, since some have passed on, and some I do not get to visit them and thanked them in person.

This book is an addition to other academic core books by Dr. Bahman Fakhraie, beside the dissertation. They highlight the new field of study about technological injections and paradigms shifts, and econometrics discoveries contributing to specific area of teconomic studies, and contribution by Dr. Bahman Fakhraie, as a new scientific teconomic series. The following books list and define areas of this new field of studies,

- Teconomics, the microeconomic aspect,
- Teconometrics, the econometrics aspect,
- Political Teconomics, and Teconomic Verbalism, focus on distributive and macroeconomics aspect.
- Teconomic Analysis an Remedies for Millennial cascading economies, applied analysis of modern economic problems

CHAPTER 1

INTRODUCTION

These writings reflect accumulation of studies, teaching and real life experiences in agricultural, academic, and automotive fields in both developing and advance economies, in applied fields as well as the theoretical dimensions. I have met a great many people from different part of the globe many of them in the USA academic communities, and I have met a great many Americans, the kindness and good heartedness, love of family and hopes for good jobs, their hopes for humanity and freedom, among all these good people is strikingly the same. However, the global views of the American people has deteriorated to such an astonishing extend, that it is vastly differs from even my mixed-happy experiences. It is an extreme view toward many hard working, self-sacrificing, non-political, generous and industrious Americans, themselves transplants from many diverse cultures.

Alas, academic work and research is hardly an individualistic endeavor, we always stand on shoulder and corps of our contemporaries' and predecessors' good and bad <u>ideas</u>, while we pretend we do it knowingly, or mostly unknowingly, society benefits as the result far more than the alternatives. All honest advanced economies devise institutional arrangements for registration (and in wiser more productive countries methods of maintaining, rewarding, and utilizing) the new creative reconstructions to benefit capital formations and add to wealth of their nations and sometimes add to global level of living. Despite the immodest objections of the imbeciles, it is either the acceptance of the scientific methodologies or dark ages, since the Advent of positivism. Otherwise, we may give it all up for the more lucrative fiction markets [the dime novels?]. Moreover, add generously to the growing supplies of the junk media, all copyright protected bland junks. The constitutional laws designed by the real scholars of democracy that signed it {not some of current misguided ones, whom like nothing better than to sign it way under different and topical pretenses}. The constitution still protects the legal right of all mortals {we the people, (all people, not just white citizens or rich citizens, or the Jim Crow right wing corporatist revolutionaries to exclusion of all immigrants and all minorities)}. The same document protects the rights of all to publish and benefit from their writings in transformative, critical, creative writings. This is in hope of discoveries, which may or may not save us from our innate capacity to engage in genocidal self-destructions, under foolish notions and stupefying implosive self-delusions, beyond true motives of self-defense and against prolonged humanitarian catastrophes, using a growing nondemocratic, dictatorial, elitists' and exclusive decision-making circles. After all, the sharp edge of reason against Hitlerism and Stalinism was utilizing legalized means to adopt their militaristic inhumane system to brutally first isolate (profiling) and then harm and destroy by detention camps and mass killing of widely defined groups of people. President George W. Bush in two states of union speeches of his first term has noted most dangerous "isms" to modern civilizations: Dictatorial Totalism, Hitler's Nazi-isms, and Stalinist's Communism among other versions of the State-isms, and the non-state Terrorism. Of course, we need to add Colonial Hegemonic Mercantilism and the old Euro-Imperialism to the same dusty discarded piles of human history. Because they operated like plutocratic monopolies under set of rules, which laws become tools to carry out elitists' exclusionists' wishes? Rather than hold up humane principles with the widest ring of inclusionists' agreements, formulated out of the chaotic rankling of many interests, with checks and balances for any functioning democracy.

Some have proven not to uphold their pledge of office to uphold the constitution and bill of rights. The institutions, which cannot perform their duties "to defend" but their duties can be an agenda to undo "we the people" and other elements of USA constitutional laws, in favor of office feudalism for institutional rogues. Those with such few bills of tenders or bash and grab laws need to reconsider for a more constructive higher path. They say they are anti-terror, but they are found to advocate a little bet of torturer here and there and not always in field of battle. We need to be absolutists about both terror and torture. To suspend the very freedoms and laws to terror blindly and indiscriminately, and to apply the jack booted version of laws to large portion of population or religions aimlessly and endlessly is to harm commerce and civil society. It is to finish the terrorists' jobs for them. Our best hope is to reduce the supplies of what fuel terrorism by our deterministic respect for human rights and humane laws that we already poses, and sometimes forget or ignore, beside the strong defense at work. Every time we pick innocent individuals and abuse their constitutional rights, to invade their privacies to plunder through their banking and finance records without accumulated distinct links and the constitutionally required legal police work, and substantiated probable cause, and justifications is to further the cause of the terrorists by many fold. It is to reduce the meaning of civil societal laws by many folds. Just as when, we murder by legal process minorities and others while innocent, by mistakes, by prejudice, or laziness, by prosecutorial jingoism, , which we all have become mindful of in the push for death penalties, as a society we further join and sink to the level of those isms by gradualism or by greater degrees. These denigrate the hard work of great many meticulous and overworked government employees, lawyers, public servants. When we allow lawlessness and torture in our great institutions we have gone past the slippery posts and slopes, and slept off the back of the honey wagon, and we are in the honey well of history. If we are there aimlessly or by bad designs, even if there is a crowd there, that is no comfort to the wiser democracies.

One of those important capital-formations inducing law is the following principle of "fair use act" in protecting scholarly research. Another antidote to the "creative destruction," since it is an incomplete non-constructive mean by itself.

United States federal law under Title 17, of United States Code (Section 101) defines the "Fair use," following is the shortest version,

> "Fair use is a reasonable non-infringing use, including reproduction, of copyrighted material for such purposes as criticism, comment, news reporting, teaching, scholarship or research, as determined from consideration of all relevant circumstances, including (1) the purpose or character of the use, e. g., for commercial purposes or for nonprofit educational purposes, (2) the nature of the copyrighted work, (3) the amount and substantiality of the portion used in relation to the

> copyrighted work as a whole, and (4) the effect of the use upon the potential market for or value of the copyrighted work."

Beyond the "fair use" and "brevity" implications, please let me know (author of works, others with legitimate legal documentation of copy right with reasonable time limits from initial date of publication, or 14 days, by signing and mailing the two pages of permissions letters (From Indices). If your rare-great contributions to humanity beyond the scribed laws, have been over used. It, the transgressions, will be corrected promptly in the next publication of the same great importance (or in the web page if available at the time) and /or replace the source. Otherwise, if you want to be mentioned, or have a forward, well I try to read everything, as time and other resources allow, please, sign "the permission letters" (from indices) and mail it with your requests.

Electronic means, #2 Pencil makers, and yellow note pads deserve general thanks, from most writers and researchers. They are the infrastructures of research, they are too ubiquitous and helpful to ignore. Electronic mediums also assist in such progress, and thus they get legislative licensing and access to public for a fee to be helpful. That is well deserved aside the rare but infamous occasions, when monopolistic licenses become harmful tools for predations; after all we are in the age of spy-wares. It is unfortunate that such good means and laws are targeted by greed and hubris of some commercial entities and their paid for treacheries. In particular, when they violate privacy laws and worm their junk materials without permission unannounced on others' computers. Then they get litigious with children, grand parents, students, and teachers, compounding their treacheries with litigious terror and aggressions. After failing miserably to self-regulate, no wonder, they want their version of tort reform and libel limits now. The two items [#2 Pencil makers, and yellow note pads] could have claimed all the fame of helping progress and writers, and for a long time they did.

Teachers, professors, colleagues, helpful friends deserve much more than they receive. We truly find the value of their contributions to national and global wealth when they are replaced with robotic unoriginal automaton morons whom believe democracies are set of rules for everyone else but them. Moreover, greed is a constructive philosophical paradigm by itself, or their personal media-myopic views from the bottom of trash hip give them more universal vision, rights, and voices, more than the constitution and laws give others. Worst yet is to witness, the academia being attached by sub-intelligentsia under newer pretexts and modern bugaboos to force their firings or silence, by presumption of guilt or tonnage of <mess> media accusations.

Alas, a gracious “thank” to all teachers seem to be the least I can do for most of them. In addition, I need to remind everyone again all errors are mine. The corner stone of learning is not being perfect! Nevertheless, it is making errors and trying to fix imperfections around us, one question at the time and nine failures for each one success. Omar Khayam a Farsi poet, shared his vision with these words of wisdom about humanities dreams and their failings, here I reworded them in translation:

"What we walk on is dusts of imperious kings and kingdoms,
Gracious humanitarians or despicable despots of their days,
Super powers and self-proclaimed perfections of glories

Step gentler, humbler; do not gallop irreverently,
You pour droplets of the aged wisdom-wine or bloods,
On humanities' dusts and your broken -dreams,

There is no doubt; we are the next dust-layers."

Hence, the wisdom of the prophetic phrase:

"Seeking knowledge and learning, from cradle to the grave."

It is not without recognition and extreme sorrow and condolences to all the aggrieved, that recent years' events leave us observing the deterioration of human conditions around us. It is with hope that such vicious economic and financial cycles in Africa, the East Asia, and South America and globally do not induce any or further loss of fortunes or lives. That improving human conditions encourage respect for human lives, human rights, and economic wellbeing regardless of people geographic locations, or citizenship status, and their theological inclinations if any. Indeed, if any entities do not believe in a set of core human dignities and human rights (or a global bill of rights), which all humanity deserves, they deserve more global scrutiny and enlightenments. The more intense analytical study of our galaxies so far show this earth is the only vessel afloat with all of us on it, how well it stays afloat is indeed a global and fundamentally non-military academic and intellectual recognition of hope for decent life for all, by all.

Equally unsettling, is when theological moralists presume there is morality without ethical foundations, or without any universal understood core of human values and ethics. Atrocities and human degradations inflicted on civilian population often women and children of any religions are terrorism of the worst kind. I cannot even imagine any deity, which advocated or wanted fears in the eye of children or defenseless people. No piety or religiosity can advocate harming civilian and noncombatants to dominate them or change their minds, rob them of their properties and lives, or even encourage imperialistic and dictatorial fascism as false salvation, at least not again at this day and age. No mater, how quickly or fastidiously one builds on wrong innovational foundations, the risks of ruination increases with the speed of construct. If the African pandemic in poverty, and AID, or any old colonial Euro-constructs to be repeated, and duplicated in Asia unabated. The humanity will witness its quickening deterioration on one of two paths: one, a Dante's nightmare of thermonuclear proliferation and abuse, or the other, a Malthusian and Dickensian diameters of sickness and poverty spreading globally, engulfing and overtaking wealthy nations even with their advanced technologies and weapons, and wealth.

The sooner we get on a sound constructive humane path, on the improvements path for all humanity to engage in productive helpful endeavors the better all of our lives will be. When we get there, we will still have the issue of sharing it all. Moreover, how to agree to disagree on growing hosts of issues. If we cannot advent comfortable solutions acceptable globally now, it will not get any easier with all the squabbling. Here and in the few books, I will present the other half of scientific yen and yang arguments of the last two millenniums, the new creative constructions mechanisms needed to complete the creative destruction mechanisms presented in innovational changes and relatively free market structures and for functionally democratic governed economies.

Technological Advancement

Technological advancements are the progress of sets of knowledge and skills used in new production or productions of new capital (human and non-human), new goods and services.

Progress of technology is not just the result of individualistic curiosity of inventors or scientists in an intellectual vacuum. The economic variables are among a host of stimuli that now guide institutional interest in technological advancements.

The logic and application of scientific discoveries and its by-products technological advancements are not as understood phenomena globally as one would conclude from the coverage. Most governance value but misunderstand the wiz bang by-products of the process as a process in itself The process of technological advancements is not as sleek and clean as it is portrayed, nor is as cheap and without negative side effects. These would require expensive and time incentive remedies for corrective actions.

Societies have faced is to use an example. The way an orchard with different fruit trees are cultivated is such an example. Invariably wags, village experts, and some concern cultivators will tell you their opinions about, , which tree to cultivate, while the wealth of the nation (village) is in cultivation of all trees with values reflected in the market demand for their fruits, all trees, which the variable climatic conditions will allow you to cultivate.

The most erroneous perennial argument is the one when certain item in the budgets ends up with 20 to 70 percent of national budgets, while the systematic process of

Advancements, technological changes, the educational infrastructures all depend on 2 to 3 percent of national budget for their basic competitive survivals. The recent arguments over such requirements are illuminating among European advanced economies.[1] The OECD data shows; United States only has spent 2.7 percent of 2000 budget, on research and development. Japan spent 3 percent of their budget. But, the European 15 nations are not even close to spending enough on technological advancement, and more alarmingly is that the level of future expenditures are even more puzzling, "The United States spent 2.7 percent of its 2000 budget on research and development and Japan 3.0 percent, while EU nations have lagged behind since the mid-1990s, according to OECD data. The United State government also plans to increase spending by more than 20 percent over the 2001-03 periods, and Japan's budget has also been expanded"

> . . . It is important to realize that the United States is dramatically more successful than the EU in

> attracting young talents at the post-doc (post-doctoral) level from all parts of the world"

The other serious dilemma is where the funding is spent. Agriculture or defense getting disproportionate and irregular sums from some governments is hardly indicative of organized and constructive growth strategies in technological advancements, when funding of education and university system go anemic, or when certain branches of government find pretexts to advance contradictory policies.

In the analogy of orchard again, different trees need maturation periods of a few years up to five or seven for stone or circus trees. In the meantime, while certain groups discuss the virtue of eating ripen fruits, other groups cut the trees down and use it for firewood even wet, before it gets to bearing fruits. In the meantime, what would best enrich the village, or nation would be, to cultivate the orchards let them get to fruition, and as the trees get closer to the end of their productive lives arrange replacements of younger tree in their place to best maintain constant supplies or increase supplies to existing markets. This gives a new meaning to the old school story, in teaching the young students by planning a new walnut tree among many old and productive trees. In addition, reminding them that those who planted the old orchard may not be here to eat or supply them the products, however, they planted them anyway, and so this generation can eat and enjoy the result. Abundant productive tree will not be there unless generations after generation plant and nurture them.

Capital stock of the nation like in the Persian-walnut tree school story will not be there to create jobs, upgrade infrastructure, sustain generations, without deliberate nurturing and attentions. Humanity has manufactured their lives with certain advanced complexities, which if ignored will undo relative progress, or even influence their survival.

The important realization need to be subsumed that the economies are not agrarian, material and capital used are complex and have multiple uses or useful life spans. Break points, obsolescent, replacement points can be decision-making points in time that may or may not coincide normally. Adding to that mixtures biological limitation of operators and the need for computer failsafe over ride operations increase the need for alert recognition of manmade complexities injected in operational productions.

In such a complex fog, it is common for uncommon ideas to gain unusual supports, alas the unholy marriages of robotic and computerization and non-conservative extreme right ideologies have all the earmarks of birth of postmodern market fascism. Its anti-population anti workers elements are global and astonishing, in ignoring the demand market dimensions. Governments even advanced economies can fall victims to its many appeals, bribes, money wealth concentrations instead of wealth creation, and its other contortions of realities around us.

Governments are interested in the increased productivity and economic growth, thus the partial impact of technological advancements on potential increase in the level of living. Private firms like the potential profit attached to the same inputs' costs producing more output, leading to more sale, and possibly more profit, or the reduction in cost, which less inputs (with more productivity) producing the same output will yield. Therefore, potential markets influence resource allocation and investment in new and appropriate technology generations from applied and basic research. Before an invention can be used and lead to economic growth satisfy national needs, or be supplied to advertised-induced consumer demands, it must undergo its metamorphosis.

The new idea must be perceived as a marketable good or service, be applicable to a production process, or become a new machine with other old and new parts. The process is a very expensive one. Often, old capital must be discarded before full depreciation has taken effect, while a risky new way is tested for feasibility and profitability. Thus, the need for increased saving and investments or upwardly adjusted investments should be clear.

In addition, there is a need for functional financial market (credit market) to allow economic agents (entrepreneurs) to do the needed conversions of capitals' many forms.

In addition, the economy, which can risk much of the resources, must already be financially a sound and functioning economy. Fiscal pressures in instabilities and distributive imbalances will influence sustainability in the longer run.

The Derived Demand For Technological Advancements

The derived demand for techno-advanced goods and services is the sum of segmental demand for goods and services with embodied and disembodied technology by consumers and other producers and the derived demand for technological progress in the production process, for capital in use and innovation, by entrepreneurs and producers. Then the demand for inventiveness leads to the demand for inventions, research, and scientific activities.[2] That is, theoretically inducements (through market mechanism) are assumed to get to the entrepreneurs, innovators, and inventors. This may prove to be a difficult argument in cases that disconnections exist, between market rewards and individual creations and production.

The one segment of the economy determines the ultimate success or failure of technologies supplying goods and services. The most dominant purchasing power (70-90 percent) of the gross national product is made up of consumption in a market economy. Producers are the other economic agents most utilizing technological embodied and disembodied goods and services used in production of other goods and services, as long as there are demands for the byproducts.

Despite the importance of technological advancements (embodied and disembodied in human and non-human capital) in development of the history of human economic growth, this is never the main economic reason behind the demand for them? The demand for products and services by consumers and producers combine to make up the formidable derived demand for technological advancements.

Reduced Price and Techno-Progress

Consumer and producers both respond positively when they can use any new product as a substitute for higher-priced commodity, service, and input, or if they get a perceived-improvement subject to their current financial constraints. This is especially useful if the new products from technological advancement are very useful so they increase employments, and their price decreases, therefore, there are double boasts to income.

Computers use and their involvement in work had exploded over the last three decades. Government issues personal computers licenses to operating-software of the computers. They can become government issued monopolies. Therefore, the price of software at $80, or double the competitive market value of $40, may not appear to have a grave impact on the market. Nevertheless, a large portion of the population can be kept out of learning and participation for the additional $40 per product. Two decades later, it takes from $90 to $600 and additional monthly fees to connect to the system, still large portions of the people can be left out of the system, only for a short period of time. They will show up in social unrest, incarcerations industries, at a ten times the costs of education per student. The telling statistic is that the latter industries are growing!

The 50 percent, deference per product could have been partially taxed and properly fund the public education, retraining the displaced workers, without robbing everyone and keeping them in ignorance for political gains or expediencies, and expounding the great constituency of idiocy, and the real zero sum games of the greedy incarcerations-industries. In the balance, the owner of patents or copyrights would have become multi-billionaires at a slower rate. Alas, if shareholders had more of a share in such fortune building initially, perhaps the negative impacts would be more dissipated. Yet, we see when governments fall short of tax revenues, good will of multi-billionaires can hardly compensate for national and international deficiencies caused by inadequate revenue distributions, real jobs, and real incomes of the population.

The prices of personal commuter have dropped from unaffordable to semi-reasonable a price for a personal computer or lab top under $1000. However, the same cannot be claimed about the common languages (software) of the Personal Computers hard wares. In addition, to all of the new must-have gadgets that will inundate business activities, this software will add high initial introductory costs.

Consumer Demand

The most dominant purchasing power of the economy, the consumer demand, is guided by consumer utility function. Thus, consumers would be induced to buy the kind of goods and services, which would be within their sets of budget constraint.

The byproducts of process of technological advancements (invention, innovation, and capital in use) must meet the same criteria. That is, the new good or service must be priced low subject to the consumer budget to allow attainment of a higher indifference curve or produce a low-price substitute to what makes up the consumption basket. Alternatively, produce such a novelty item would modify the taste of the consumer. In addition, it must be within consumers' income constraints, it must be within the budget.

Techno-advanced Price Reductions of Commodities

The most recent and vivid example of modern consumer durable product of technological advancement of many combined scientific fields is the personal computer. A many-roomed big multiple mess of wires, and bulbs, costing many times the annual revenues of the world's biggest institutions and nations were called computer in the 1970s. Most households and students had no access to it.

Comparatively, now in the 1990s, a nicely packed mix of computer chips and a few short cables, a desktop personal computer is available, priced less than the average monthly salaries of an employed advanced-economy worker. Clearly, for the consumers who prefer such an item, the technological innovation embodied and disembodied in the personal computer has made it possible in two decades to have something they could not have before. They still are able to buy other items in their consumption basket. There are still high-priced computer systems in the world, but the choices and the alternatives have increased at the end of this technological advancements process.

Another vivid example is the price-impact of inventions, innovations, and capital in use related to agriculture. In the history of early colonial America (the eighteenth century), the same imported technology was used in agro-production, which was mostly for familial consumption.[3] In the Europe of the eighteenth century and in present rural India, like most rural agrarian life of developing nations, it takes 50 percent of income to obtain food.[4] By contrast, 10-20 percent of average income of an employed worker in an advanced economy is allocated to food. This allows for more of the income to be allocated to education, skills, human capital accumulations, and transfer of technologies to individuals.

Techno-advanced Price Reductions of Substitutes

There are number of commodities in most consumers' baskets, which are substituted for others as seasonal price changes occur. When prices of a close substitute are reduced due to technological advances, consumer demand for such commodities can increase.

The present consumer demand for home central heating/air condition systems has increased consumer demand for gas versus coal. In fact, demand for a commodity (cable, for example) will change directly (increase or decrease), if some technological advancement changes the price of a substitute commodity (VCR, for example). The cross elasticity of relative demand for a television would be positive with respect to the relative techno-advance price change of the VCR (videocassette recorder).[5]

Techno-Advanced Price Reductions of Complements

Technological progress also affects consumer demand of complements. These goods are commodities used in relative fixed percentages of demands for each other. The demand for television sets will increase if innovations changed reduce the costs of electricity. Alternatively, the demand for a VCR changes if the price of the videocassette changes. The cross elasticity of relative demand for VCR quantities would be negative with respect to the relative techno-advance price changes of the video cassette.

Techno-advancements and Consumer Taste

In earlier history of most advanced economies, in most developing nations, and in some countries, unless consumer taste it is changed, much of byproducts of technological progress, may not meet sufficient demand to sustain their development and use.

A large set of exogenous variables (sociological: education, culture, politics, theology) to economics may affect the endogenous variable demand, via consumer taste to halt or expedite technological progress. This is one reason to explain the faster rate of technological change in the utilitarian colonial America versus British custom-tailored demand for consumer items.[6] The existence of the phenomenon shifts much of the earlier focus of inducement for innovation adoptions from producers' isolation and suppliers' base to a demand and supply base inducement.[7]

The initial geographic dispersion of familial, rural America with accumulated land and livestock imposed certain needs for transportation and information. The general store, Montgomery Ward and Sears & Roebuck ordering catalogues, likeness of Ford's Model T to horse buggies all preceded modern advertisement and auto industries.[8] The importance of consumer taste has led to multi-billion dollar producer-supported advertisement industry. The purpose of the public relation advertisement industry is to modify taste and preference of consumers, thus consumer demand for goods and services. Many sets of psychological and communication innovations are so financed to modify consumer demand. Another way of looking at this is to remember your first computer and those floppy disks. You use to exchange and save, now look at your laptops, with hard disk storage of 80 gigs (giga bites), and CD storage disks with 700 kb (kilo bites), memory card, flash card of 4 to 16 gigs, if only you had stayed in college to learn something to write about the globe in flames around you.

It is important that when a culture has taken an adoptive and utilitarian position in her tastes and preferences toward an innovation, such an innovational progress has taken effect. In way of explanation, an adoptive culture may have reduced the risk factors facing entrepreneurs on their way of supplying novel ideas or products. It stands to reason, not to further risk presenting new ideas. If every new idea has a 50/50 chance of getting you either killed or bankrupt. Nevertheless, if the novel idea gives you the same odds for financial rewards beyond your dreams or some financial losses, you will risk more often. This also may explain the relative economic growth of more democratic economies.

TECHNO-ADVANCEMENTS AND CONSUMER INCOME

One of the most important byproducts of technological progress and availability of cheaper goods and services is the relative increase in income to consume and invest more. The choice made will directly affect the future income and level of living. Take the example of the reduced cost of food in an advanced economy. Assuming that 20 percent of workers' disposable income is spent on food, a large sum of individual resources is left for shelter, entertainment, and improvements in his consumption basket. Perhaps about 80-90 percent consumption expenditure of the disposable income, leaving 10 percent for education of the households as an investment or saving for future consumption and investments. Firms or the governments in most economies pay health often contractually, because it plays such a big role in the competitive productivity edge most advanced economies are seeking.

Infrastructures are often ignored abstracts until they become national or international disaster points, a source of shame, a cause of many deaths. National and international investors in capital in any economy will have more than second thought about having their own assets in jeopardy in system that undercuts its infrastructure funding. Local or federal government can ignore and under fund bridges and roads, until a bridge pancakes and many lives are lost, in bright day light.[9]

> "The collapse of the eight-lane Interstate 35W bridge into the Mississippi River on Aug. 1, 2007, killed 13 people and brought immediate calls for repairs to bridges across the nation.

> The failure to follow through was not because of lack of effort, officials said. Soaring construction costs, budget shortages, election-year politics, a backlog of bridge projects, competing highway repairs, and bureaucracy often held bridge work to only incremental progress."

Education, basic and retraining, is also gaining recognition due to its role in productivity increases in the internationally competitive markets. If there is such a large allocation of available income for consumptive goods and services (entertainment) over investment in education (10-80 percent), one should also see a re-allocation of resources and national foci. Such a miss-allocation of resources and national foci is not hard to find. Refer to the author's work "Hollowing Headless Nations on Taxation and Education," and many excellent publications about the American high-priced athletic ventures (multi-million dollar contracts), and under funding of infrastructure for education, food and shelter, and roads, and schools are available. That, next to the massive under-funding of social program related to retraining and education (and United States average income of $42,600. 00(@ 2002)), and the salary packages of United States business executives, (500 time the average salary), and current legalities. Try to keep a straight face, when the next right-wing moralists tell you we should copy current business for educational improvements models. However, consumers are also supplying work input to the production process, which is becoming more responsive to an innovation-using ever more competitive international market.

The producers would only pay high income to the workers who are constantly increasing their self-embodied human capital by education and retraining. Perhaps it is an easy skip from this logical need for skilled worker to the paradoxical argument that robotization will replace the need for workers. While this is no longer a technological impossibility and aside from the politics, such supply side dream-logic is confronted with the basic need for, workers' income-demand, thus workers' demands to buy the products. If all workers are under employed (unemployed) in all segments of the economy, the economy cannot afford the demand for high-priced innovational junks. Alas, mindless market mechanisms have been known to do significant damage before, market or governmental breaks and modifications have been adopted to control the damage. As the rate of technological changes speed up enough, the potential for such deviation and externalities will become significant.

The technology products like other commodities can be either normal or inferior goods. Since the dynamic aspect is the issue, the innovation byproducts should initially be a normal good, and later, an inferior good.[10] That is, the demand for such a commodity should increase with increases in income, then fall. Therefore, the income elasticity for number sold with respect to real disposable personal income over time should be positive for new products, but negative, when they products become obsolete or other novel and useful commodities replace them. For the most part, 1940-1970 has been an important innovational period for passenger cars, initially uncomfortable, now a balance of electrical, combustion and other multi-systems of technological advancements have been a prize-purchase of the American consumer. In the following table 1, the income elasticity of real disposable personal income and number of passenger cars are studied. This table also reflects the positive attitude of consumers about the technology embodied and disembodied

Table 1 shows the number of car sold per one-dollar increase in disposable personal income.

Table 1. Income elasticity of consumers for cars.

Year	1940-50	1950-60	1960-70
Elasticity	3.95	.004	1.52

Note: Real 1972-dollar disposable personal income and numbers of passenger cars sold are used in these calculations.
Historical Statistic of the U. S. 1967, Statistical Abstract of the U. S., 1967. Economic Report of the President 1984.

This economic index shows the amount of interest that exists in the marketplace, for the products of new technological methods of production. Therefore, the post war demand for cars was greater in 1940-50s than 1ater. Moreover, it peaked up again in 1960s for car replacements, and the new generation purchases.

In application of the same economic measurements to number of agricultural products are even more interesting. The income elasticity of consumers for these numbers of agro-products show a positive index and peak for complementary new products and a negative ebb in index for the substitute or obsolete product. As disposable personal income of American agriculture base families increased, the more they spend on new more and productive machinery. In addition, they spent less on traditional modus operandi on farms. Later, since the percentages of people on the farm also declined for larger-scale operations, urbanization, and international suppliers, the indices also changes for some innovational machinery over time.

Recently, we can study our tendencies for replacing new cell phones, by mini computers multiple communication devices. Dropping the old breaks phones and landlines for smaller versions. Alternatively, offices are becoming mobile by laptops, (i-pads, i-phones, cell phone, androids, etc.). These have now migrated from the technology geeks, to Wall Street types to college professors and educators.

Table 2 shows technological index for agriculture production tools from mule, horses, and livestock days to modern machineries.

Table 2. Income elasticity for innovational products.

Years	IE: DI & Tractors	IE: DI & Combines	IE: DI & CornPickers	IE: DI & Animals
1940-45	1.3	2.5	1	-0.4
1945-50	6	12	23	-4.7
1950-55	1.6	2	3	-2.5
1955-60	0.5	0. 4	1	-1
1960-65	0.08	-0.5	-0.5	N/A

Note: Real 1972-dollar disposable personal income and numbers of farm animals are machinery are used in these calculations. Economic Report of the President, *Agricultural Statistics, 1967*, 1984.

PRODUCER DEMAND

Producers will be motivated to take risks, borrow, and invest in the uncertain outcomes of technological advancements if they perceive some profit potential from the above mentioned vast consumer market demand for innovational and novel products. The profit formula: Profit equals revenues less costs.

The producer to increased revenue must find customers or other producers to sell more output to them. Better products and new, innovational methods to produce these or older conventional commodities produced better and cheaper do help. Nevertheless, for the reduction in costs, the producers must have cheaper and more productive input or a cheaper alternative to his present input or a better combination of input to produce more, which means better production techniques to reduce costs. In the above table farm producers, among others, comprise different market demands for novel products used in production of other output.

Increases in economic activities in different businesses are assumed to induce more concentration of innovational work. The increases in international demand for electronic imports from Japan has followed by an increase in Japanese patents in electronics.[11] Changes in family size, urban-rural mixes, economic growth, are among the variables, which may influence profitability-risk potential of technological progress (Rosenburg: 1972, 40). Some other changes in population growth and the age compositions per capita income growth, change in related innovations also can affect demand for innovational works.

<u>Producer Demand and Techno-advanced Price Reductions</u>

Producers, entrepreneurs facing the same profit formula and risk prospects tend to choose least-costs appropriate production techniques. Since they are kin to market price mechanisms, they would upgrade their production method with respect to relative prices. Thus, American homebuilders would use more wood relative to the British or Middle East builders, which use more brick or masonry.[12] Naturally, more invention may target least-resource cost appropriate techniques to guide their innovational talents.

Institutional Demands-Induced Techno-progress

Governments during wartime, universities, and corporations now regularly finance research and development. It is true that in times of war, military needs induce many such demand-pull inventions.[13] While the institutions may have a general wish and wish lists for certain technological advancements as supply-push invention, they do not have little direct control on the creation of inventions.

Their means of directing inventions may be freedom to research, finance the researcher or a team of researchers, collect relevant information for the team, and reduce risk and increase reward and incentive. In the case of governments, allowing for stable but responsive systems of governing allowing innovative changes to take place, but also be present in case of negative externalities of technological progress and market mechanism failure.

Some of these factors are in use already. Government regulations are applied in patent systems and copyrights are used to protect the inventors and other creativity, anti-trust laws are used to reduce monopoly market blocking.[14] While the constitution assigns the task of copy rights laws and protections to congress. The important task of fair use, allowing responsible scholars to criticize, rebuilt, transform, erroneous or bad or trite and outdated works, and science falls on congress. Without such latitudes and protections, no new or important discoveries will be magically appearing in any culture. The danger looms that well paid for lobbied laws reflecting the interests of multi-billion dollar monopolies, void of the voices of others including scientists can easily legalize theft of individuals, scientists, writers, and creators' services.

Cook the golden goose of creativity in an economy that still does not fully understand this process.

Some military and quasi-military institutions are financed for their inventive productivity and the diffusions of products. DOD and NASA are a few famed examples. Government support of civilian technological progress also exists, whether it is in guaranteed buy of products or in winning of contracts. An example would be the financing of some avionic innovations of post-WWII by the United States and other Western economies.

Governments can be internal to the economic process. Central banks, treasury and trade regulations may play a far more pivotal role in investments or imports of appropriate technologies, and enhancement of market mechanisms, yet unexplored, or transforming ideas to product phases of product developments.

Notes

[1] Tue Dec 10, 9:40 AM ET, London (Reuters) - Europe's leading scientists criticized the European Union's science policies, calling for "funding to curb further brain drain to the United States."

[2] Rosenberg: 1972, 3

[3] Ibid,

[4] Schultz: 1981, 4

[5] Stigler, George J., "*The Theory of Price,*" 3rd Edition, (New York: The Macmillan Company, 1966, 31-34

[6] The acceptance of standardized machine-made but quality products in America allowed for customer versus producer based inducement for technological progress and mechanization. Rosenberg: 1972, 43-44

[7] Schumpeter: 1939, 73, and Schmookler, Jacob, "*Invention and Economic Growth,*" Massachusetts: Harvard University Press, 1966

[8] Rosenberg: 1972, 48

[9] CBS news, February 11, 2009 2:33 PM, America's Bridges Still Falling Down, http://www.cbsnews.com/stories/2008/07/31/national/main4309822.shtml

[10] The percentage change in quantity sold is taken relative to the percentage change in real disposable personal income. The more standard definition of normal and

inferior goods and income elasticity is available in economic literature. (Stigler: 1966. 33-34)

[11] The change in economic activity in an industry is positively correlated to relevant changes in patenting, with time delay. Schmookler, Jacob, " *Invention and Economic Growth,*" Massachusetts: Harvard University Press, 1966

[12] Schmookler, Jacob, " *Invention and Economic Growth,*" Massachusetts: Harvard University Press, 1966

[13] The Manhattan Project yielded one of the most complex inventions of human history: access to atomic energy. Its good and bad potentials are still ongoing. The invention of synthetic rubber instead of South East Asian natural rubber is another example. Ibid, 42

[14] Ruttan, Vernon W. , "Usher and Schumpeter on Invention, Innovation, and Technological Change," *Quarterly Journal of Economics*, Vol. 73, 1960, 596-606

CHAPTER 2

THE SUPPLY OF TECHNOLOGICAL PROGRESS

The supplies of technological advancements are identified as two initial types. One is the set of knowledge, which must further be defined as basic, and applied scientific knowledge and inventions. Two is the set of skills and qualitative improvements in basic inventions in order to apply them in the process of production. Innovational changes and improvements, informed of new capital (human and non-human capital, i. e., new machines, and tools) are of the latter kind. Thus, the more general definition of technological advancements is used.[1] That is, the progress of set of knowledge and skills used in new production or productions of new capital (human and non-human), new goods and services. The new hybrid grain, or pest-resistant seeds, new marketing, managerial skills, financial development, or another electronic time saver would meet the definition of technological progress.[2] The post-Schumpeterian focus of economists on the post-innovational phase (and solely creative distraction) may have clouded some judgments, leading to resource miss-allocation away from other phases of appropriate technological progress and the assumptive requirements of economies for sustainable growth and development, as they are developed here. For an invention to end up in the form of final novel new products (good or service) or a new production process, it must go through the qualitative process of innovations and capital in use phases.[3] Schumpeter (1938) excluded invention by definition from his model, stating innovation possible without new inventions. Nevertheless, P. A. Usher's revised work was published after Schumpeter's death, and made such exclusion unessential. Thus, if the patent-holder innovator is unable to use it in production, other agents must be induced to do so after purchase of legal rights to it. That is, innovators and scientists must first supply the new idea-invention. Then innovators and entrepreneurs would take that invention or a new combination of older inventions, and apply them (as new capital in use) to supply a new product or a new production process to produce an old product.

Inventive Process and Supply and Techno-Advancements

The contribution of inventive process to supply of technological progress is explained in view of two factors. One is the synthesis of practitioners' methods with the scientific methodology. Two, is the discovery of inventiveness process.

Internal logic of scientific discovery reflects motives for understanding. While practitioners' motives for technological change was for use in production.[4] Historically, practitioners would discover their skills without knowing the scientific logic of them. It has been noted that extensive innovational changes can take place without any new inventions, often based on new combinations of old inventions. However, the synthesis of technology and scientific methods have speeded the rate of technological change. In addition, the complexity of new discoveries, mostly concentrated in the research of applied science, where financial resources can be spent on teams of researchers focused on certain problems.[5] When the expected benefit and probability of enough profit-induced resource allocation to the targeted problem, where the rate of relevant technological advancements tend to increase.[6] In fact, over the last two decades, the federal government and industries spent more than universities on research and development programs.

Next, the inventive process is presented, which can explain the emergence of a new idea and the development of ideas to inventions, innovations, and capital in use as a process of supplying technological progress.

Emergence of Novel Ideas

The subject of much fascination, novel ideas have been studied by anthropologists, historians, and sociologists before applied scientists, economists, and econometricians. Cultivation of constantly coming up with ideas is not as common as everyone assumes. Perhaps, because mind is always busy, some presume all their mental thought-dribbles are great ideas. Training idea-development into useful patterns of products, through inventions-innovations are truly the essences that make wealth of the nations, if the nations finally grasps the meaning of such processes and how to cultivate them. Some cultures and nations learned to cultivate such endeavors in themselves and immigrants and such cultures flourish. Some cultures and nations chose (sometimes suddenly in reaction to internal or external shocks) to shun any new ideas, immigrants who may bring them, the new mechanisms educing changes, they even institutionalize it, such culture either weather and die or stay stagnant while the world zoom past them. In history, such cultures were left behind clueless and their population saw waves of progress pass them by. These universal afflictions have befallen on all countries and cultures in different times. They happen to all religions, and sometimes they are brought to some countries exogenously.

The Transcendentalist Approach

Novel ideas were given mystical and inspirational attributes and were left to intuitive acts of genius.[7] Practical ideas were guarded to death, as divine secrets. They were passed down from fathers to sons, or from Magi to Magi inside temples, for most of ancient human history. Theologically, they would be revealed to high-ranking religious peoples. Secularly essential truths would be passed to inspired aspirants as people of rare natural gifts to a very select group. The Persian princes (16 to 6 BC) in line for the crown had to undergo a ceremonial ritual designed to reduce their numbers, before they were trusted with the governance methodologies and high office. They would attack lion prides with short swords and lance in small royal numbers.

The process of supplying ideas would become implausible if our graduate students or even creators of bad books, movies, and extreme left or right strategies were systematically, dropped in the lion cages for their new questionable ideas. The market place is a financial lion cage for all bad ideas. Continuity of productivities demands that it should not be as lethal. Nevertheless, then again if you have no job or health insurance, it becomes a matter of polemic indifference between immediate terminations versus prolonging inevitability. That has to be remedied.

Ralph Waldo Emerson (1803-1882), as leader of New England Transcendentalism explained "transcendental forms." Emmanuel Kant (1724-1804) defined these, as an important class of ideas, which come by intuitive thoughts rather than experience.[8] The approach failed to explain the cumulative additions to collected human knowledge and critical reason over the historical long run. Therefore, insightful acts are not as rare or person-specific, as they were once imagined. Moreover, specific-problem pre-conditionings increased the possibility of such relevant acts of insights.

THE MECHANISTIC APPROACH

The process of creation of inventive ideas as an accumulation of small parts or portions of the whole idea accumulated over a long time, and then put together in a much larger useful whole of an idea.[9] The stress and tension generated out of need for a new idea would help make the process of creating it to happen.[10] Given advancement in knowledge and social relation and the cumulative synthesis process, these make the whole of an inventive idea to be accumulated and piece together. This approach has been credited for, one, the cumulative synthesis of many smaller parts, two, for presenting it as a long process.[11] However, this approach does not present the details of the process. The explanation is underrating the role of inventors. It is assumed to have a deterministic certainty.

THE CUMULATIVE SYNTHESIS

This approach is the middle of the two extreme processes. It is divided into two segments. One is the creation of individual insightful acts, which may not be an inventive idea. Two is the cumulative synthesis process, which is a combination of more insightful acts with many other ideas and parts toward forming a whole, having a more probable chance of being a strategic invention.

This would be the most likely process of creating inventive ideas, because multi-sociative synthesis of ideas would be concentrating and converging in this process. Alas, it will not explain the essential and continual fine-tuning characteristics essential to democratic processes intruding constantly in the process.

The Gestalt Theory

The Germanic Gestalt pattern is used to explain a formed whole whose parts belong together and have a quality to them in that organized whole, which is different from juxtaposing the same parts randomly. The founders of the Gestalt theory were three German psychologists: Max Wertheimer, Wolfgang Köhler, and Kurt Kafka.[12] Inventions, as whole organized forms (Gestalten) are a massive synthesis of smaller whole insightful acts, which are syntheses of other acts of insights.[13] The social process would yield us a close circle when initially there would be incomplete circles (i. e., David Kaz: proximity, closed forms). Kafka stated laws of maximum simplicity, regularity, and symmetry would help the stimuli to yield a good psychological organization (Gestalten).

Köhler experiments show a chimpanzee using a tool placed close to food to retrieve the food while no previous experience existed. Kafka identified the act given the setting of the stage as an act of insight. Arthur Koestler draws a parallel: Archimedes already had the problem in his head before his bath. Thus, the combined mental fields became one and the solution was not invented, but found. Running without cloth was just theatrical effect, or marketing flare, we are still writing about it.

Thus, by setting the initial proximal stimuli combined "in space and time" they would form a certain kind of predictable perceptual organization, that is, an act of insight.[14] Then a social process for invention exit, which does not depend on mystical impossibilities nor systematic determinism and can account for historical progression in mechanical technologies. There are four sequential phases in the initial process of emergence of novel ideas or emergence of insightful acts. One is unfulfilled wants, needs, demands, or an incomplete pattern would initially present the problem. The need is to focus the of individuals' concentration.

Two, is combination and collection of initial relevant information to satisfy the need and fulfill the demand. The practitioners very early used fumbling, trial and error at this stage, which pure chance playing a big role.[15] Later, the scientific method and organized experimentation with a more probability for success were to lead to relevant acts of insight. However, not all conditions and information may be available for all possible people. In addition, people may be subject to a number of forces that make them unsuccessful.

Three, the relevant insightful acts presents a solution. Therefore, the solution is found by chance so an exact timing of such activity is not possible nor there are assurances that it would take place every time in a deterministic or mechanical fashion.

Four, this phase is for critical study, revisions, thus mastery of new ideas. The new idea then is a 'technique of thought or action."[16]

It becomes more important if it useful with the rest of experiences and cultural accumulations of the group. The accumulation of such events could then lead to inventions and the process of cumulative synthesis.

Primal needs for food is a very basic demand, which Gestalt psychologists noted. In the history of human development, the set of needs have evolved to more complex issues. This can be a great start, but as an explanation either it falls short of the real life, or the importance of inventions have attracted much more resources and focus for economic reasons, either way, the regularity of applications and existence of inventions and innovation in modern economies requires further study.

IDEAS ACCUMULATION, CUMULATIVE SYNTHESIS

Accumulation of ideas and improvements in communication cross-cultural and over time increased the rate of cumulative progress of ideas. The process of organizing the related ideas to a relative whole that constitutes an invention is called the cumulative synthesis process.[17] While V. W. Ruttan identified the second and fourth steps needed in innovation, the distinctions between the process (the emergence of a novel thing or cumulative synthesis) were not made. The same was also true about E. Mansfield's (1971) presentation. A.P. Usher (1954) found the cumulative synthesis as the source of any inventive creations. Nevertheless, the dynamic cumulative synthesis would be even more likely to yield appropriate innovation. It is a collection of the four steps in emergence of novel ideas, combined with a large number of old and new inventions, ideas, experiences into a massive synthesis process.

This process explains how the scientific need for pure understanding and discovery of the supply-push argument is combined with the institutional and economic need of the demand-pull argument in formation of a strategic invention.[18] That is, the scientists' need for discovery can play a role in the desire to complete the incomplete pattern in the process.

In addition, it explains how the institutional funding and economic needs become relevant to the setting up of research teams and are internalized to the social process of inventions. The massive synthesis process is to be used by practitioners, inventors, innovators, and scientists.[19]

However, the injection of practical and exogenously corrective decisions, or the adoptive signals are unknown in this processes or steps. We can deduce the critical revision phase may be for such refinement. When improved ideas, some learned on the job, some learn from exogenous education are added during this process.

The Cumulative Synthesis

The perception of incomplete pattern is another phase. This could be the result of innovators' need to use, or the scientific need to discover, or the institutional area of focus to understand and improve a process. While individualized means of measurable inventions have been on the decline, individuals (even in team research) play the unique role to the process.

Setting up the stage phase is another step in innovational processes. The recent requirement for research is more complex. The individual researchers have large sums of human capital invested in them. They are self-financed or state or federal capital invested in them. Then the institutional infrastructures for the research to take place, needed equipment are also parts of non-human capital for the setting-up stage.[20] Thus, financial needs of researchers and the institutions become internalized in the social process of cumulative synthesis, and societal allocation of resources become deterministic, when international competition is involved. Nevertheless, all of the preliminaries should be cleared and all the data and information pointing in the direction of invention ought to be collected. In case of a major invention, all relevant past inventions would be already available.

Industrial research laboratories and agricultural experiments stations are two American examples that have utilized these facts. The establishment of experimental laboratories was a clear recognition of benefit from the applied process.[21] Alas, regardless of Henry Ford's background as a bicycle technician and availability of information on horse buggies. Still, it was Henry Ford and none other who invented, innovated, and utilized resources in a unique way to make the Model T car.

The act of insight phase, as part of cumulative synthesis, it implies a special act of insight in combining other inventions and acts of insights lead to a new invention. Thus, a more complex process requires some knowledge of previous inventions. A more complex learning process of previous knowledge is suggested. Henry Ford could understand and fix a bicycle. Bicycle repair induced no one else to invent the Model T.

The critical revision and mastery phase is also a part of cumulative synthesis. Failures serve historically important services, and A. P. Usher internalizes them to the process on creating novel things. Assuming the errors are documented and studied, or they are repeated enough as norms to become obvious practices.

There may be inventions or scientific works already discovered but not used or applied. Because the fourth phase of cumulative synthesis has not applied to them. It could be after other inventions and future critical revisions occur, then the full mastery of other new inventions takes place. If we assume the revision phase is saved for all modification, it may be too late in the process for many changes. The modifications needed here are reflective of changes in modern economies to allow for financing the activities, which are both extensively costly and risky about their ultimate market-abilities.

Dynamic Cumulative Inventions-Synthesis Process

They dynamic cumulative synthesis process would repeat the four steps, while the set of novel ideas and inventions are increasing over time. A. P. Usher introduced the first and second phase as parts of the second cycle. The historical relevance of having few strategic inventions for any socially important achievements was known.[22] For example, the personal computer invention took place after relevant electronic inventions, use of digital numbers, and audio-visual communications were already invented, before the earlier personal computers were available. Table 3 shows the different categories of funding research and development funds.

Table 3. Total R & D funding and categories. (Millions of 1982 $).

Category	1970	1975	1980	1985
Total R&D	62407	59883	73237	96999
Fed. as source %	57. 1	51. 7	47. 2	47. 9
% of GNP	2. 6	2. 2	2. 3	2. 7
Basic/total R&D %	13. 7	13. 7	13. 5	12. 9
Fed. as source %	70. 2	69. 2	70. 2	65. 7
Applied/total R&D %	21. 9	22. 0	22. 2	22. 6
Fed. as source %	60. 2	57. 4	55. 5	53. 1
Development R&D %	64. 4	64. 1	64. 3	64. 5
Fed. as source %	55. 4	48. 5	42. 6	45. 0

Note: Total R&D includes basic, applied, and development funds. U. S. Bureau of the Census, *Statistical Abstract of the United States*, Washington, D. C., 1989, 577.

Further inventions have added to the expanding base of personal computer knowledge. Besides the continuity of the process, the inter-disciplinary and intra-disciplinary discoveries have further increased the rate of technological progress.[23] There are social benefits not accounted for in the private firms' returns or in the researchers' returns.[24] The table above shows the diminishing federal funding of research and development. Therefore, there is a need for governments' allocation role to finance research. In fact, the table 3show the value different advanced economies have given the invention process in their economies by allocation of non-defense research and development funds to advancement of knowledge.

Some arguments favor anti-immigration laws and delusions of constitutional laws to enhance growth, among a canned list of misfortunes as they occur unabated, or induced to occur. That would do little but shut off the capital mobility to the American economy, while baby--boomers portion of population will explode and wage earners and real wages have been manipulated to be kept low, with worker unions confronting governments and semi-government group attacks to erode their influences. When the minimum wages are occasionally raised 10 cents for the working poor, you hear political voices everywhere about the implosion of the economy, about inflation it creates. you will not hear the rare few political voices, or any sound laws to remedy against looting capital markets by the executives' wage-packages at more than 40 times, 100 times, 200 times, or even 500 times the national average income (@$42,600 for 2002) of the American wage earners.

It is astonishing that first amendment and fifth amendments are the only part of the USA constitution understood by the media, the employees of the same and other executives. The media never saw the wage package of new privileged executive subclass jumped from 10 times to 500 times more than the average American earnings in the two decades it has been happening. Since, the last half of sixteen century colonial Americas' working conditions of American Indians, slaved Blacks, and indentured whites, no such outrages class division and poverty creations have gone unseen with such deliberations.[25] Often, we read history and repeat our past mistakes, rather than learn to avoid them.

The sound policy would deal with the knowledge advancement needs and fill the Research & Development 50 percent gap, so that United States businesses can compete on an equal level. Because eventually, the advancement in knowledge leads to innovational entities in the very competitive international markets that can compete and dominate or take market shares. This is different from monopoly domination of markets, or military types of domination both are drains on the economies and too exclusive to be constructional in modern economy rebuilding strategies. Since 1976, improvements have been made but the following table should alert the comparative need for resources in advancement of knowledge as a step to technological advancements.

Table 4 shows percentage of fund, which goes to Research and development of nondefense technologies. The leading funding often goes to military related industries. In most economic advancements, unless the technologies are readopted, and converted, they will remain useless to economic advancement.

Table 4. Percentage of non-defense R&D funds for the advancement of knowledge in some advanced economies, 1976.

Type	United States	U K	France	Germa ny	Japan
Non-defense R &D to Advance Knowledge	8	37	37	58	56

Note: This is calculated from Mansfield's defense share percentages less 100. The data excludes U.S. general university funds. Dates cover 1974-75 Japan, 1976 U. K. 1976-1977 U. S.[26]

Experimental spirit part of entrepreneurship makes inventors or academic mavericks, which are important and unique to the invention process, as entrepreneurs play an important role. They alone, or as a team, are those with the inventive-insightful acts. That is, their endowed human capital would specifically make them unique and valuable. The costs of the human capital, higher education, and training, books, educational and trade periodicals have increased above all others.

However, all other costs of maintaining a family also have increased as reflected in the growth of disposable income, GNP, or inflation, CPI. Moreover, the relative value of teachers, professors, researchers have declined with respect to others, whom are perceived by youth of a materialistic society as viewed and valued members of that society, thus paid accordingly. That is, a definite allocation of private national resources that has taken place contrary to the best interests of the whole, as noted in this study. In fact, that is why education has become such a fundamental point of technological competition push for the future. Nevertheless, no longer a private, small-funded venture can really turn around the national economy of any nation.[27] At least, they cannot affect it enough to meet, compete, and lead international class-multinationals or the giant-industrial market.

There is a current scientific evolution two decade or so old, in theoretical particle physics shaping about the older subatomic (+) proton and (-) electron hypothesis as essence of mater formations to smaller entities the ubiquitous neutrinos and an estimated trillions is supposed to pass through earth each day [and the possible counter neutrinos]. Now that it is proven that neutrinos have mass, courtesy of Japanese $ 81 million, 10 billion yen investment in the (2002) Nobel Prize winner, Tokyo University physic Professor Masatoshiba Koshiba's project. In this project, huge pure water tank (about 10 story tall called super- Kamiokande stored under grounds away from the sunrays) planted with light measuring devices.[28] The potential are great if even extremely small impacts on other subatomic particles are caused, or energy releases can be measured. If the scientific community could measure material entropy due to neutrinos', mass bombardment and find solution to counter the material decay. The Microbiological implication if neutrinos energy bombardments and induced gene mutations can serve other academic fields. Did such an energy impact contributed to multiple or diversified humanoid-origins.

Yet, other implication for theoretical physics can help us understand energy loading of subatomic elements enough to alter particles Oxygen to Ozone, or even better yet to reverse such a process. At this level, science no longer can happen on an individual financial capital but individual knowledge capital still is needed, and very productive. Scientific projects of this type are rare. In addition, it is rarer to have small economies, which can afford to finance them. However, commercial-technological products may materialize up to three decades later, if ever in later in some cases.

The developing nations have also increased resources to these endeavors. A large list of developing nations, which have allocated increasing amounts of financial resources and scientific person-hours have sustained some growth in their economies.

The internal and external barriers are far greater in smaller developing economies. Table 5 shows real per capita annual (RPCA) growth rates in government agriculture spending (71 U. S. $) and scientific person-years and GNP (84 U. S. $) in developing nations.[29] Table 5 shows growth rates in Agriculture, scientific hours, GNP.

Table 5. Growth rates in Agriculture, scientific hours, and GNP.

Countries	Gov. Av. Spend. `54-74	Scientific Man Years `54-74	GNP `75-85
Brazil	32	32	1. 27
Columbia	2. 5	11	1. 58
India	5	2	2. 52
Indonesia	62	115	1. 25
Korea	11	4	8. 23
Mexico	11	14	1. 31
Malaysia	10	22	4. 71
Pakistan	3. 2	4. 2	4. 06
Sri Lanka	2	5. 6	3. 76
Taiwan	6	0. 6	4. 27
Thailand	15	13	4. 27
Turkey	15	41	1. 37

Note: Population estimated from the U. S. Abstract and others.

The real per capital growth rate per year of expenditures on agricultural research in the Islamic Republic of Iran were 28 percent, 1959-74.

The scientist person-year per capital per annum growth rate was 4.4 percent.[30] These have been duplicated in many different nations as the importance and science in the process of inventive and innovative synthesis further discovered.

The extended explanation of dynamic invention cumulative synthesis process was to restate:

1. It is organized, and to some degree more continual than first thought.
2. In the case of institutional and mechanical inventions that are patentable, and the creative and scientific works, which are issued copy right, the invention base set (basic knowledge and creative works) is

increasing. Therefore, their potential use will be increasing, too.

3. Make explicit the unique value of the inventors, researchers, experimenters, and scientists with the creative human capital to this process of dynamic creative (inventive) cumulative synthesis.
4. Governmental protection of their ownerships, much as the property rights and agricultural productivity, will have a positive effect on the future productivity in this area.
5. The intellectual property ownership rights of the individual are opposite to those of some politically and financially powerful interests, or some institutions and governments.
6. Ban laws calling intellectual enslavement, neo-peonage acts.

Since, the inventors' roles are valuable to the whole of human societies. Specifically, there is a law targeted by the institutional interests (PACs), which aims to pass the right of ownership of intellectual property rights (i.e., copyrights, etc.) from the creators to the institutions where they are working as part of labor salary contracts and in addition to their works performed for hire. This should be called intellectual enslavement. It should be dumped next to the unfortunate communal agro-productivity experiments of our starving international neighbors, and peonage practices of the past, because it is a direct attack on inventive-productivity motivation. The institutions know the motivation.

The Economic Report of the President stated "Thomas Edison, after unsuccessfully trying to sell his first invention (an automatic vote counter), vowed that he would work only on ideas for things that people would buy."[31] International protection of intellectual property rights was such an issue on the administration agenda.[32] There has been a decided shift away from rights of ownership to institutional control. That we will find to be an intellectual dead end for dynamic societies depending on individual invention energies as much as any advanced economy must depend on such inventions and multitudes of creative solutions of different kinds.

Innovation Process and Techno-progress

This process is a special class of dynamic cumulative synthesis process.[33] This is not in Schumpeter's theory of innovation.

In this study with a new dynamic cumulative innovational synthesis (DCIS), different from the dynamic invention cumulative synthesis process, the speed and direction of innovation also are influenced. Given there is no guarantee, an increased probability of breakthroughs exist. The statement of V. W. Ruttan (1960, 604) may clear some issues.[34]

"The focus of conscious effort to affect the speed or direction of innovation centers around the second and fourth steps in the process as outlined by Usher–in setting the stage and in critical revision. By consciously bringing together the elements of solution–by creating the appropriate research environment–the stage can be set in such a manner that fewer elements are left to chance."

In addition, the planning phase of what is in J. A. Schumpeter's theory of innovation.[35] Economic agents study the old and new inventions, innovations, insightful acts, and different sets of economic feasibilities, in order to establish the potentials for a new production function.[36] So planning for new factories and new equipment, new innovative firms and old innovation-generating firms and entrepreneurial spirits in risk-taking (other than financial risk-taking, unless new ventures are self-financed) or experimental spirit are also essential for the innovational process. Alas, the formulation fails phenomenon of new ideas like the computer microchips evolutions into industry-computerization of business, governments, and educations, without any significant a priori road maps.

The design and building of a new factories and rebuilding of older ones, exist the chance for the adoption cost-reducing innovations, available inventions. There are two cases, which may require more explanation: the issue of duplication of factories and replacement of old parts of a factory may not include innovation.

The duplication of factories involves innovation, if it occurs at the early part of diffusion and adoption phase of innovation, if it is in a new market, a new region, or a new country. Moreover, at any time, it occurs by the use of newer, more innovational production techniques, new innovational factory reorganization, or innovational marketing strategy, to affect supply curve of the same factory. There is less innovation involved, in the case of a duplication of a product, at the end of its product cycle in the same area, in a saturated market by other suppliers.[37] There is little to be gained from the innovation residual in such a market, unless that rare innovation increases the profit over the average costs of production.

The replacement of old parts, with the same identical parts, made at the same way and same costs would certainly constitute no innovation. However, new parts made of better material, which would last longer (i.e. use of steel for iron) made much cheaper would entail innovation, inventions. Often, the number of patents issued and copyrights registered are used to measure the effect of creative and inventive efforts.

However, patents on new inventions are sometimes used for innovations. New legal entities representing the entrepreneurs do engage in innovative ventures. The legal entities are sole ownership, S-corporations, C-corporations, or trusts, which conduct all business activities. Alas, they would normally engage in innovative actions if they plan to set up new factories or build new equipment or design new organizational relations and marketing strategies. The innovative older firms, which have maintained an inner innovational team, will succed.[25] They systematically engage in economic competition, through innovational process. The distinction is drawn between, competitive capitalism and "trustified" <institutionalized> capitalism, when sizes of the firms are in question, in Schumpeter. There is a good chance that the "giant" firms (i.e., monopolists, and multi-nationals) could engage in non-economic means (legal, etc.) to stop entry or shut out innovative smaller firms to certain markets. While they will have to compete with other big firms their own size by more innovation and by economic means. At least, they might, due to fear of retaliation, or extensible regulatory involvement.

The following table 6 shows the numbers of copyrights and patent registries in United States.

Table 6. Annual growth rate of patents issued by categories and copyrights registered.

Years	Total Patents	Foreign Corp.	U. S. Corp.	Individuals	U. S. Gov.	Registered Copyrights
60-65	6.6	14.7	6.7	4.6	4.7	4.1
65-70	0.4	10.4	- 0.14	-3.2	2.6	1.5
70-75	2.6	9.8	-1.2	5.6	1.8	5.4
75-80	- 2.8	- 0.1	- 2.9	- 4.5	-9.4	3.1
80-85	3.3	9.0	1.3	-0.06	2.0	3.2
85-87	7.9	12.3	3.9	9.3	- 4.5	3.9

Note: Column 3 includes patents to foreign governments. Data includes patents for designs, botanical plants, reissues. Source, U. S. Bureau of the Census, *Statistical Abstract of the United States*, Washington, D. C. : 1974, 1985, 1989.

Unionization of labor movement regionally was designed to introduce leverage (advantage) in wage package negotiations to counter negative cycle generating income concentrations and chronic demand-deflationary cycles. In addition, they introduced a human element in a machinery of production process. It is when these balancing mechanisms fail to accommodate a sustainable aggregate demand in the macro economy. Here the true values of economists whom are knowledgeable about other monetary and Keynesian tools are recognized. The United States' anti-trust laws are frequently cited in such cases.[38] Others, big or small, will naturally die out if they do not adjust by constant innovations to the changing economy conditions, in that case fall prey to sub-case condition of "Schumpeterian creative destruction."

The Entrepreneurship

The economic agent entrepreneurs discover new economic possibilities where none existed before, they perform economic insightful acts in the dynamic cumulative innovational synthesis process. Classical economists did not recognize the role of entrepreneurs, known to J. B. Say, profit was the capitalist's share only. It emerged after the marginalists' revolution again. Moreover, the neo-classical economists noted entrepreneurs' role and profit in the 1980s. However, it disappeared from the theoretical work. The study of theoretical works by J. A. Schumpeter and F. Knight reintroduced the subject to economics again.[39] The entrepreneurs with the injection of innovation and production methodologies will change the consumer satisfaction obtained [in demand terms], and the yield derived [in supply terms], from resources, mutatis mutandis in any given period.[40] They behave in a manner specifically different from other economic agents, because they will break through the traditional modus operandi, the conventional ways of thinking. They are involved in all innovational economic activities. The entrepreneurs' skills make them uniquely aware of the relative economic possibilities around them, either for a short period or they may choose to keep informed of such relative economic conditions, laws, and social phenomenon relative to their economic activities, such as people as specialists in each such field would learn to do. The entrepreneurs' decision set resembles his awareness of the economic and non-economic conditions around him. There are shorter versions of entrepreneurial characteristic, as capital < financial> market arbitragers, which miss defines both agents of capital formation process.

However, we will see the processes involving the transformation of choice ideas to applicable technologies, and successful production processes and economic ventures are far too complex for individuals unaided and non-synchronized to conduct with balance the economic purposes of national or integrated global economy. The 1920s, 1930s, cyclical deflationary implosions, in the West, 1980s military-costs implosion in the East, repeated financial meltdowns on cyclical bases are such examples.

They are not assuring testimonials of our academic understandings, or appropriateness of our technologies transferred, and the yield derived [in supply terms], from resources, mutatis mutandis in any given period.[41] They behave in a manner specifically different from other economic agents, because they will break through the traditional modus operandi, the conventional ways of thinking. They are involved in all innovational economic activities.

The entrepreneurs' skills make them uniquely aware of the relative economic possibilities around them, either for a short period or they may choose to keep informed of such relative economic conditions, laws, and social phenomenon relative to their economic activities, such as people as specialists in each such field would learn to do. The entrepreneurs' decision set resembles his awareness of the economic and non-economic conditions around him. There are shorter versions of entrepreneurial characteristic, as capital < financial> market arbitragers, which miss defines both agents of capital formation process.

However, we will see the processes involving the transformation of choice ideas to applicable technologies, and successful production processes and economic ventures are far too complex for individuals unaided and non-synchronized to conduct to balance the economic purposes of national or integrated global economy. Some historical epochs tell us so, The 1920s, 1930s cyclical deflationary implosions in the West, the 1980s military-costs implosion in the East, and the more recent repeated financial meltdowns on cyclical bases are a few prominent proofs.

These are not assuring testimonials of our academic understandings, or appropriateness of our technologies transferred, even if the democratic political mechanisms were ready to take constructive advice. Nerve mind, the counter constructive mechanisms of monopolistic plutocracies, monarchical dictatorship, or superficial military democracies imposed on the developing economies.

Dynamic Planning and Product Development Utilizing New Technologies

A transformative application of product life cycle planning and budgeting by author yields to the dynamic and sustainable development of new products. This process utilizes new and appropriate technologies.[42] In this model sales of at least two products (a, b) are used as an example of two level of technologies reflected in methodologies producing (a, b) over time. The phases of are divided into different stages to make the process a manageable series of events[43] There are certain variables and characteristics to look for in each phase:

1. Phase 1, initial development of product phase: The sales of product increases at different rate, initially at increasing rate enough to encourage the added costs of

research and development, advertising, and high labor and overhead expenses.

2. Phase 2, growing of new product sales and production: While the sales will be much more than in the initial phase, the point of inflection in this phase goes from increasing of sales at increasing rate to increasing sales at decreasing rate. The capital market is approached to finance production expansion. The research and development focuses on production technologies issues. However, the funding becomes available to study product differentiation and new product development. If that skip this stage, it will become essential in the next phase. The process generates Jobs.
3. Phase 3, Product maturing phase, Some shops or small businesses stay in this phase, they also pass it on as inheritance, unless or until they completely shut down the operation. In larger operation, this becomes the takeoff phase of a new firm. They present it for public

shares and apply the generated access cash flow to launch product differentiations and new lines of products as they expand. The phase start when the sales revenues are growing but at the decreasing rate. Still the sales are higher than before, but the second mathematical differentiation start being negative. The employment rank increased, and salaries and skill improve as well.

4. Phase 4, shut off or expansion decision phase, this moment comes to all operations. For managerial team or owners of firm the profitability of operation the need to cut losses, or make a graceful exit are ongoing concerns, but the sales of product start decreasing after zero growth for a time, and they start to decrease at increasing rate. The options in new markets or technological changes are few or unsuitable for conditions faced by the operation related to product (a). However, the hope and options related technologies and

product (b) are either expanding or also declining. Therefore, the sum of net revenues generated are increasing or changing directions. If there are net revenues from both operations take a negative turn, the shut off plans need to be implemented. Alternatively, mop up operation after the shut-off phase, are orderly closing down and termination.

5. Phase 5, the follow up phase, in revisiting phase 1, a successful product (b) will require the same actions but perhaps with most new technologies, retooling and retraining for new skills. Larger institutions do create such flow of inventions and activities, and they can raise the needed cash flow from the capital market to enact their plans. The research and development internal to the businesses usually yields such great returns.

The net earning potential line can also represent profit from the two endeavors (a, b), however, the operational and related expenses taken out can differ in different firms. There are some very peculiar notions about implications of excessive wage packages. It is assumed they are good to be kept low at the lower ends, and limitless at the top end. Both notions are unsustainable, the former, for starving the economy, and the later for looting capital markets, and shareholders shares. The latter, can prove to be far more distractive and receives the least political verbiage.

Figure 1 shows dynamic, sustainable products-development phases, using technologies (a, and b).

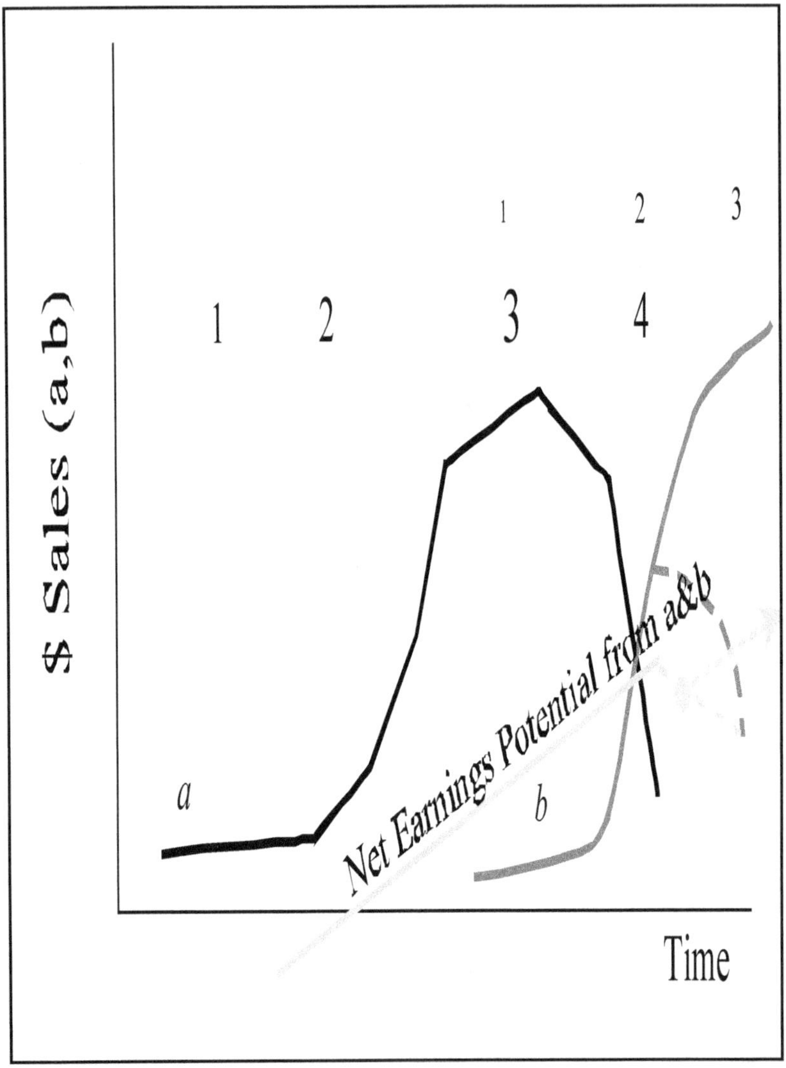

Figure 1. Dynamic-sustainable products development (a, and b).

Earnings, Net Revenues, Profits, Capital Formation

Unless there are earnings, most operations are terminated, or shelved. Even when there are earnings, it must be sufficient to cover reasonable operational expenses, wages, and rents, purchases of overheads and machinery to justify prolonging the operation until the sales really take off. At some point, the sales and earnings increase the cash flow sufficient to have funds left over the operational expenses and taxes, which is often profit.

In most small business, this is often put in expanding the operation by purchase of more equipment or capital stocks. In larger operation, higher earnings, often is passed on to shareholders as capital gain or equity yields. The existence of earning and the degree of risk stock holders assign to each stock determines the prices earnings ratio: 7, 17, 27, and 47, which the stockholders are willing to hold on to a stock. The earning divided among the number of stocks determines the initial value of the stocks. At this phase, often-large set aside funds out of earnings goes for research and development, new products, and new markets, and purchase of new capital stocks, embodying the new technologies, or replacing older technologies.

The earning can also be looted for wage packages, and unreasonable benefits of executives. It is reasonable to argue for the following formula for limited number of executives. However, larger obscene sums are now common in millions and billions of dollars.[44] The following formula introduces an anchor- link, a sane connection between the now run away executive pays and their economic contributions. It will be impossible at this stage to do this without government further involvement in the disconnect that the corporate executives and their handpicked cohorts (boards members) have created.[45] The logical proposition having workers by their retirement funds, and executives by some stock ownership benefits share an interest in the long-term growth of companies have long been subverted for greed.

The following formula is only a starts:

Formula:

[(Y) x $ 42,600(AV U. S. INCOMES = Base Value)]

Base Value x [(1 ± Rate of growth or decay)]

{(1+ r ± 20 percent), (Y = 10. . . , 40, . . . , 100)}

For example:

(10 x $42,600= $426,000 base value)

$426, 000 base value x {1.20 or 0.80} = $511,200 or $340,800

No more than the same amounts in shares ought to be bought in open market as part of their salary packages of any executives. No options or any speculative instruments should be in such a package. Executives on their own can buy or sell options in the open market unless it is in their own company. In that case, it has to be pre announced by 6 month. Up to six year, after they leave a company (about two short-term business cycles) they ought not to liquidate their holdings, unless there is a pre-arranged semiannual plan to sell, or convert their stocks openly.

The much larger numbers in multimillions are reflective of deterioration of democracy and market imperfections now long established. They go back to Nixon-ism effect in political ethics beyond Nixon, dependencies of the same political structures and educational institutions on business funds for campaign advertisements for legal favors. An example is the abolishment of Glass-Steagall act without protective-clauses for regular customers, small investors, and voters. The depression era law made it illegal for banks (and financial institutions) to fund investing, and marketing of stocks for the same entities their customers. This also did not allow the accounting firms to consult the same entity they audit. The act established legal firewalls between activities, which aided greed, induced extreme speculations with bank customers' holdings. When the cycles turned negative, in face of unaccommodating Federal Reserve tight money policy, and business and governmental mindset of austerities and none intervention in the markets. The crowd mania and banking runs shut down investments, which under mined the capital markets and capital formations for the duration of the United State depression. When the banking, investing, and auditing interest groups approached the representatives, they had a captured audience. Most of mechanisms put in place to protect the public economic welfare have failed in a major ways.[46] Campaign funding reform acts are other golden sources of analysis of gradual deterioration of ethics and morals of politics and commerce, and sustainable damages to any democracy.

Most fast cast law patches in the recent past have been under-whelming to long-suffering (2002) stock markets; such fast laws have been superficial and further eroding to capital formation and capital market. Until, these issues are met by fast responses from the population they effect, cosmetic publicity stunts, are delaying proper repairs to market trust. Some urban centers have advanced living wage laws to maintain not only families with at least one full time worker, but also their own urban economies.

An important function of government is to accommodate small businesses and the job creation engine of national economy by tax credits or tools to allow for a national living wage law in place of the minimum wage laws. The importance of tax-spend fiscal policy is what is taxed and where it is spent. Especial clause can allow for three to six-month training period at 80 percent of that living wage law, with special attention paid to penalize abuse of mass firing and rehiring to keep wages low. There are growing portions of population, working poor, legal immigrants, and students among them, which pay taxes and get absolutely no representation what so ever. There the federal, state, and local voting rights can be amended to encourage instead of punitively charge the working poor and middle class. They can allow long-term permanent residents to engage in state and local levels. In order to increase the votes to assist the disengaged aloof systems, granted that current anti-terrorism laws – if we trust their proponents– are sufficient to protect the nation from all harmful or criminal intents, and not the pathological xenophobes, and chronic hate groups who scream and rage against legal and constitutional rights granted legal resident and citizens In United States. They are wishing for denial of women voting rights, regressions to slavery acts and peonage laws for minorities and immigrants. The like to deny any local vote rights for tax paying immigrants, while making up pretexts to deport them without any media or a real court or judges' scrutiny, especially at time of war, or other national insecurities. Hiding behind political labels cannot justify inaction on fundamental issues of work and lives of the population.

Especially alarming, is the silence of those [in leadership positions], who scream about minor increases of dimes and nickels in minimum wages for working poor and growing hordes of the un-insured workers. However, they are dismissal of the obscene multibillion dollar executives wage packages and their even more lucrative retirement "the golden-parachutes," which are looting and divesting the capital formation markets, and shareholders' equities, and workers retirements and sustaining damage to future wealth of the nation. Those are the kind of elected leaders, whom do not deserve to be reelected, even by hooks and crooks. They can contribute better outside politics.

Rate of Supply Injection of Technologies And Macro Economy

The rate of injecting appropriate technologies in an economy need to meet the capabilities of that economy to absorb the injection will complementary systems in legal structures and functional infrastructures and mechanism that would gradually increase actual employment without inflationary disequilibrium, and crippling bottlenecks. Misapplications of available technologies can create other sets of inappropriateness in use versus selection can also become financially crippling proposition. For example, a new technology may be useful in small sector of the economy, and its fast application can add to commerce in that region. However, as an unknown it can cause comprehension in larger sector and shut off flow of capital to a region over time.

The rate of diffusion by education can easily allow for the corrective and introductory presentation to the larger sector of the economy. Therefore, over time, actual employment and income of the larger economy will benefit and a greater good accomplished. Figure 2 shows technological diffusion and macroeconomic implications.

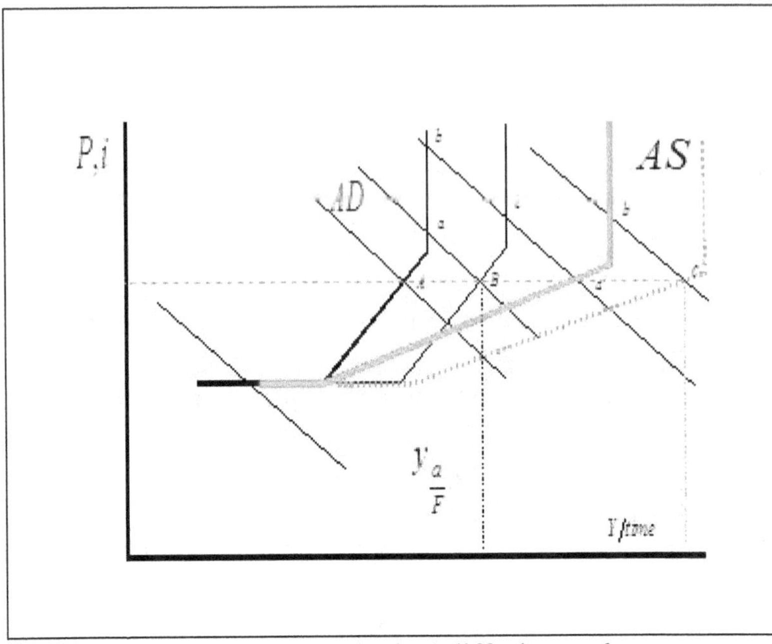

Figure 2. Speed of technological diffusion and macroeconomic implications.

In case of fast diffusion of technologies, prices and interest rate tend to increase much more rapidly in the short term. While in the longer periods, larger increase in the employment will be caused and price and interests can adjust back down. The diffusion of technological changes at slow rate will have a much larger impact on employment after the same adjustment in aggregate demand reduce the short run implication of higher prices and interests.

However, if aggregate demand remains unchanged, a deflationary phase will affect the economy.

In the region of liquidity trap, no price and interest adjustment or fluctuations take place. The additional investment in transfer of technologies will remain unrealized until the all the current capacities are utilized, but employment will increase if aggregate demand increases. Aggregate demand and incomes will need to increase substantially before price and interest are impacted.

Figure 3 shows the speed of technology diffusion and elasticity of aggregate demand implications for the economy. In the case, of income increase, which pushes out the demand, the normal expectations is that the prices will rise, thus inflationary pressures are build. However, if the supply elasticity changes with the new technological injection, and average cost also reacts and changes, you will have a deflationary impacts.

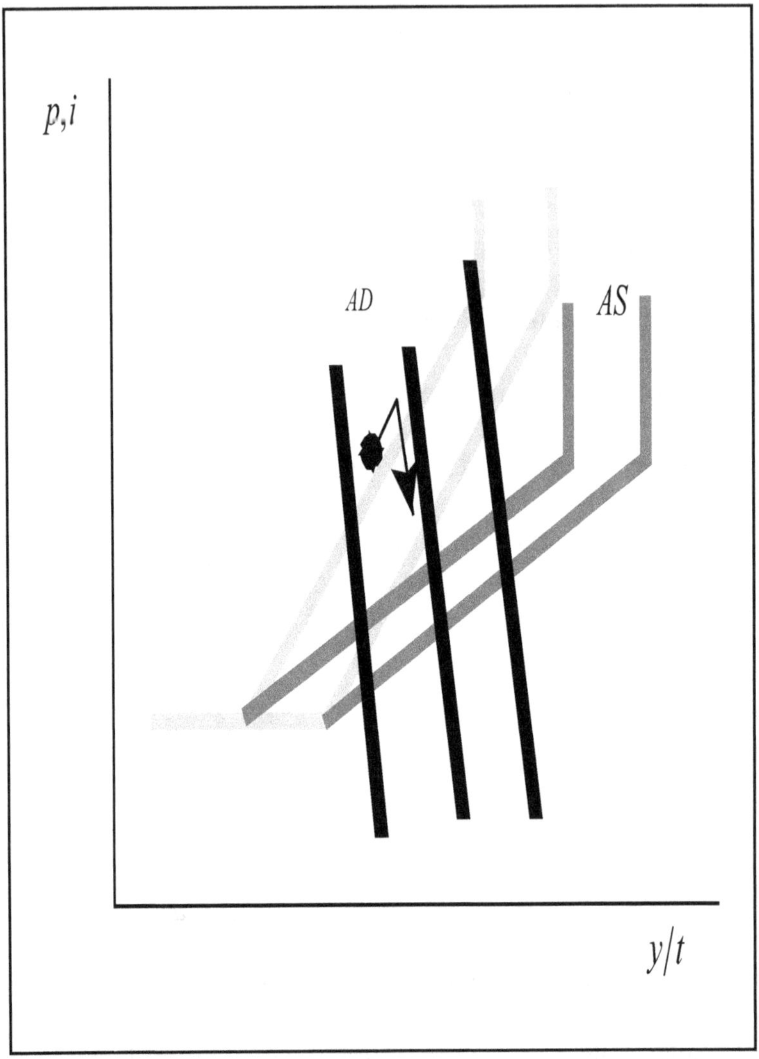

Figure 3. Speed of technology diffusion and elasticity of aggregate demand implications.

Therefore, for the governments, which have adopted a ruinous wage controls, low-income, union bushing techniques in fear of extreme inflationary pressures, this will be liberating. That with technological injection, supply curve shifts outward, and with the right supply-curve elasticity, the prices will drop.

In the region of employment trap, assuming full employment of all factors have not been met at (a), the supply injection reduces inflationary shocks due to aggregate demand increases at (b), to manageable level at (c). The difference being more employment opportunities will be created with slower diffusion rate approach as shown by (a' b' c') versus (A, B) when prices are held fixed with changes in technological advancements.

The elasticity of Aggregate demand also adds complexities to the analysis. The technological injections as shown in the figure 3 causes a reduction in the price and interest rates even when the income increases, unless the technological injections and increases in income are substantially higher. Then, P and i, price and interest both will start to edge up.

Notes

[1] Kennedy Charles and Thirlwall, A.P., "Surveys in Applied Economics: Technological Progress," *The Economic Journal*, March, 1972, 12

[2] Mansfield, Edwin, "*Technological Change*," New York: W. W. Norton & Co., Inc. 1971, 9

[3] Ruttan, V. W., "Usher and Schumpeter on Invention, Innovation, and Technological Change," Quarterly *Journal of Economics*, 1960,, 596-606

[4] Mansfield, Edwin, "*Technological Change*," New York: W. W. Norton & Co., Inc. 1971, 10

[5], Ibid, 11

[6] Ibid., 17

[7] Moran, Michael, "New England Transcendentalism," *The Encyclopedia of Philosophy*, 1967 edition

[8] Usher, Abbot Payson, "A *History of Mechanical Inventions,"* Revised edition, London: Oxford University Press, 1954, 60

[9] W. F. Ogburn, and S. C. Gilfillan, are credited for the mechanistic process. Usher, Abbot Payson. *A History of Mechanical Inventions,* revised edition, London, Oxford University Press, 1954. 61

[10] S. C. Gilfillan wrote that the invention would take place because of need and the process or individual may not be necessary. Ruttan, V.W. "Usher and Schumpeter on

Invention, Innovation, and Technological Change," *Quarterly Journal of Economics*, 1960, 601

[11] Ibid, 61

[12] Miles, T. R., "Gestalt Theory," *The Encyclopedia of Philosophy*, 1967 edition

[13] Ibid

[14] Usher, Abbot Payson. *A History of Mechanical Inventions*, revised edition. London: Oxford University Press, 1954. 61-64

[15] Ibid, 65

[16] Ibid, 65

[17] Ruttan, V. W., "Usher and Schumpeter on Invention, Innovation, and Technological Change," Quarterly *Journal of Economics*, 1960, 604

[18] Thirtle, Colin G., and Ruttan, V. W., *The Role of Demand and Supply in the Generation and Diffusion of Technological Change,* Switzerland: Harwood Academic Publishers, 1987, 9

[19] Ruttan, V. W. , "Usher and Schumpeter on Invention, Innovation, and Technological Change," *Quarterly Journal of Economics,* 1960, 602

[20] It is noted in 1900, 80 percent of the U. S. patented inventions were issued to individuals. BY 1957, the individuals' shares were 40 percent of patents issued.

Mansfield, Edwin, *Technological Change, New* York: W. W. Norton & Co., 1971, 65

[21] Thomas Edison is credited for the first research lab (1876) in the United States. Some others credit Eastman Kodak (1893), B. F. Goodrich (1895), and General Electric (1900) applied the industrial laboratory idea as a new process for inventions.
Mansfield, Edwin. *Technological Change,* New York: W. W. Norton & Co., 1971, 40-41

[22] Like the portion of savings, which is invested in new capital to generate more income, new savings, and investments and newer capital, a dynamic cumulative synthesis looks at the role of added inventions in generating inventions that are more relevant.

[23] *Frank* Lynn's study introduced the average time interval of incubation period form (1885-1919), 30 years and (1920-1944), 16 years to (1945-1964), 9 years. The rate of innovational process implies were the same or the commercial development for the same data were 7, 8, and 5 years. Mansfield, Edwin. *Technological Change,* New York: W. W. Norton & Co., 1971,76-77

[24] U. S. President , "Economic *Report of the President,*" (Washington, D. C.: Government printing office, 1990, 112

[25] Takaki, Ronald, "A Different Mirror: A History of Multicultural America,"London: Little, Brown and Company, 1993,65-67

[26] Mansfield, E., and others, *Technological Transfer, Productivity, and Economic Policy,* New York: W. W. Norton & Co., 1982, 193,
Science Indicators, 1978, Washington, D. C., National Science Foundation, 1979

[27] Part of Japan's push to generate basic research has been to quadruple their engineers and scientists from the current graduation rates of 2, 9 for every 100,000. This passes the British 10, 7 and meets the graduation rate of nine scientists and twelve engineers per 100,000 Americans. Valery, N, "Survey of Japanese Technology," *The Economist*, Dec., 2, 1989, 7

[28] Dolven, Ben, "PHYSICS", (TOKYO, November 14, 2002)
http://www. feer. com/cgi-bin/prog

[29] Population estimated from the U. S. Abstract.
Schultz, Theodore W., Investing *in People,* Berkeley: University of California Press, 1981. 50-51.
Boyce, J. K. & Evenson, R. E., Agricultural *Research and Extension Programs,* New York: Agricultural Development Council, 1975. Appendix II
U. S. Bureau of the Census, *Statistical Abstract of the United States,* Washington, D. C.,1989, 822.

[30] Usher, Abbot Payson., *"A History of Mechanical Inventions*," revised edition. (London: Oxford University Press, 1954), 68-69

[31] The Economic Report of the President (1990, 112-113)

[32] Ibid, 114

[33] Schumpeter, J. A., "Business *Cycles: A Theoretical, Historical, and Statistical Analysis of the Capitalist Process*", Vol. I. (New York: McGraw Hill Book Company, Inc.: 1939), 87-97

[34] V. W. Ruttan (1960, 604)

[35] In the following article, Usher's developments and Schumpeter theory of innovation are combined, or an explicit link between invention & innovation are made. Solo, Carolyn Shaw, "Innovation in the Capitalist Process: A Critique of the Schumpeterian Theory," *Quarterly Journal of Economics*, 1951, 422

[36] Two examples are the retailers' multitudes of stores, used as temporary occupation, European artisans' businesses, where age and tradition dictate business formation. Schumpeter, J. A, *Business Cycles: A Theoretical, Historical, and Statistical Analysis of the Capitalist Process*, Vol. I. New York: McGraw Hill Book Co., 1939, 87-97

[37] It is stated: "It is, therefore, not the new firms, which innovate and the old firms, which react, but all the competing firms, which innovation, some succeeding, others failing." Solo, Carolyn Shaw, "Innovation in the Capitalist Process: A Critique of the Schumpeterian Theory," *Quarterly Journal of Economics,* 1951. 425

[38] Ibid,96

[39] Kirzner, M. I., "Discovery *and the Capitalist Process,"* Chicago: The University of Chicago Press, 1985), 1-14

[40] Drucker, Peter F., "*Innovation and Entrepreneurship,*" New York: Harper & Row Publishers, 1985, 33

[41]Ibid, 33

[42] Byers, Lloyd L. , "Concepts of Strategic Management: Planning and Implementation", New York, Harper & Row Publishers, 1984, 194

[43] Savich, R. S., and Thomson, L. A., "Resource Allocation within The Product life Cycles," MSU Business Topic, Fall, 1978, P. 38

[44] Internet sources are subject to frequent modifications at their source.
Gordon M. , "Watchdog System Failed Enron", AP Business Writer, Mon Oct 7, 1:58 AM ET
Senate report: http://www. senate. gov/gov_affairs/100702watchdogsreport. pdf

[45] In Teconomic of Verbalism, the organizational links and impacts of this issue are studied.
Dr. Bahman Fakhraie, Teconomics of verbalism, Utah: Ferdat 2012, https://www.createspace.com/4121720 , http://www.amazon.com/dp/B00B1LO7UQ

[46] Ibid

CHAPTER 3

TECHNOLOGY, WELFARE THEORY, AND GLOBAL ECONOMY

Global economy defines around the larger national and international businesses, mistakenly or by design, it will include the larger formal and informal smaller entities, individuals (on: wheel, donkey, bicycle, motor bikes, trucks, boats, etc.) in variety of locations and shops. It includes small farmers, and their limited distribution means.[1] Globally, like locally the engine of economic activities up to 70 percent of global gross products remains in the hands of consumers, while the nexus manipulated international laws favors transnational corporations. That in itself is not a bad thing until or unless, they decidedly corrupt the systems for other users. The closest analogy is the corruption pandemic with drug cartels, when they subvert embryonic democracies or small states judiciary, with laundering and trafficking. Most profits and run quick corporate operations leave substantial instabilities and dislocated lives that over run the embryonic or non-existing infrastructures. In any such regional economies without infrastructure, technological injections need far more analysis for appropriateness. It will be much more beneficial to have local interested parties, firms, and authorities with a longer-term strategies study appropriateness of technologies influencing their lives, if the essential knowledge is honestly shared.[2] However, international systemic barriers designed by treasuries and central banks in tariffs, exchange rate difficulties, transaction complexities, confiscatory laws or dishonest corrupt practices, will prove fatal to all small regional clean transaction. The negative externalities and unforeseen effects on international commerce and exchange are also substantial. The multi-regional financial implosions of the

1990s in South East Asia, and South America, and their impacts on United States are testimonial against shriek voices of heavy-handed anti-free market regulators. While resources are wasted and scattered at all small transaction and transfer of safe nonmilitary technologies, the larger firm transactions of multi-billions constantly find legal strategies around such laws.

The other fundamental monetary difficulties with appropriate technological transfers and related capital formations are in a reasonable exchange rate fluctuations. Recently arbitrage and speculative aspects of exchange rate has passed the realm of counter cyclical balancers into financial crises creations, and economy destabilizing, beyond capacities of small governments or institutions to remedy. Again, what seems logical is to maintain small transaction currency-exchange zone by all international institution, or by varied central banks for a reasonable transaction rate, and focus on major transactions-controls, which can destabilize global banks. Of course, all criminal transactions will be subject to prosecution and law, as is and as the links are unavoidably established and required to be proven, not by assertions, but by proof.

However, greater good of free trade by smaller entrepreneurs, legitimate educational uses, health and food, and agricultural and small manufacturing productions cannot be trashed for empty boastful verbiage and unconstitutional assertions of baseless illegalities. The resulted backlash is targeted at democratization and free trades.

There is the more recent notion that presents ethno-theological monopolies, mainly sociological anomalies other than "ethnic hate" as proof of capitalism failings in a large number of developing systems. Alas, as a sub-case study of monopolies in market and political arenas there are many anomalies examples of inappropriateness of economic and political technologies transferred to developing economies. Relative perfect competition and democratic mechanism are still primary and secondary condition required for sustainable economic success.[3] There are other certain assumptive corrective requirements essential to avoid these endemic ubiquitous system failures. That is why these complex mechanisms of dynamic appropriate technological advancement are introduced.

Income and Substitution Effects of Technologies

The study of sustainable development refocuses new resources at serious global issues. Water use, energy source and use impact on global warnings, health and food (feed) shortages, or miss allocations, global population explosions in post regional wars, are not new problems.

However, the recognition of the magnitudes and speed of collective impacts of mainly consumer oriented technologies and production processes on minimum sustainable bio- diversity is so pronounced and immediate that it cannot be ignored without consequences. This is not meant in an alarmist's way, that life had changed behind hope as in nihilistic polemics, but some species have already paid for this with their lives in permanent vanishing acts.

Therefore, doing nothing, and not even studying the matter is a foolish notion. Abusing resources swill not help, especially if they are in an style induced by "madness of crowd" and mass media hysteria and "herd runs, or stampedes," by wasteful world war revisionism, militarism beyond defense and clear dangers, by government size waste fraud, by destructive bends and movements leading the financial impulsions common to leadership of the last millennium.

Perpetuating famine and medicine resisting bacterial diseases and other viral infections AID, hegemonic bents, related violent moves, and counter moves are not glory-ideas, which humanity would easily and readily survive intact. Such silly delusions and other miss-interpretations of modernity need more contemplation in true democracies and free intellectual environments and sound international laws and courts, which will need to be reintroduce globally.

If current level of production were produced with early 1900 technologies, the level of death from pollution and lung diseases would be much greater now. It would even astonish mindless apologists of the worst kinds of capitalism, as it did in the coalmines of United Kingdom or industrial smog of North East United States and England in early stages of industrial expansions. In some developing economies, this is visible now. The following model explains this phenomenon.

Figure 4 shows income and substitution effects on technological change. Therefore, at E4, there may be less toxic breathable air, then at E'4, for a nation on the budget lines, and expendetures.

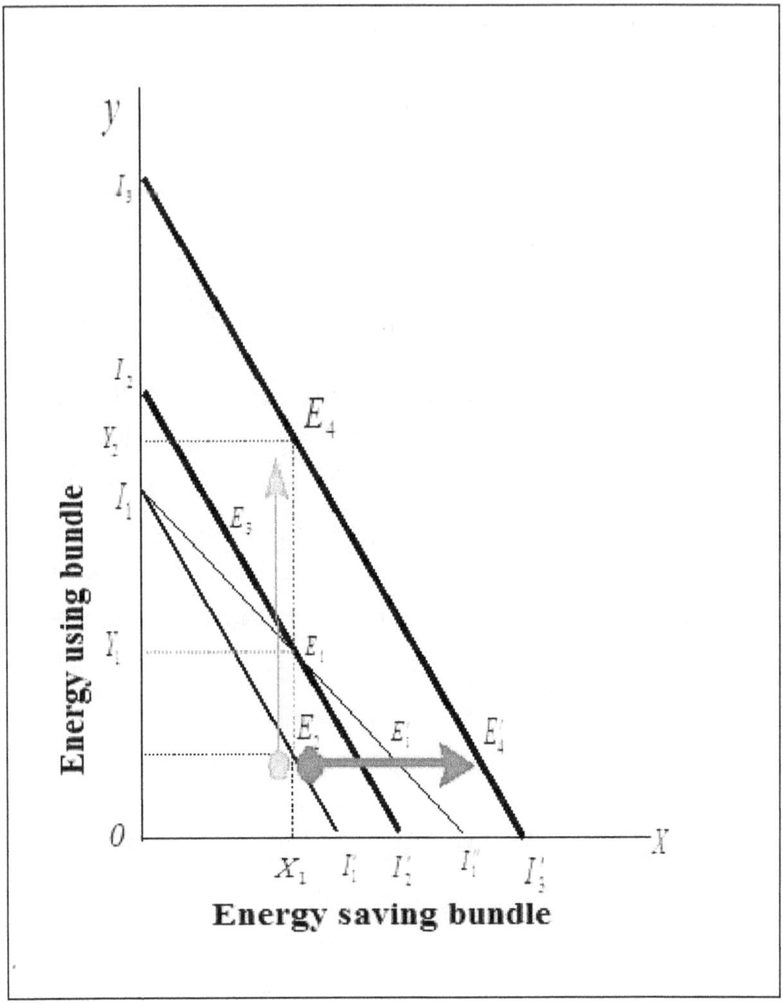

Figure 4. Income and substitution effects of technologies.

Nevertheless, technological changes have had evolved in the same two nations and others gradually to less polluting and toxic production processes and better level of living. with multiple, infra-structural supports and substantial transformation of resources and human capital form across the globe with substantial number of new technologies in the form of institutional arrangements, new laws, private property protections to fortify the otherwise illusionary sustainable development out of growth.

The X bundle of goods and services reflect the older technologies, requiring increasing usage of carbon base fossil fuels, more polluting than alternative processes or methods. The Y bundle of goods and services are more appropriate and less polluting technologies, smaller liquid-gas (propane, or butane) cooking or water-pumps in more villages and rural settings, better automobile engines (H-cell or dual fuel), and cleaner factories in larger urban cities. Initially along budget line $I_1 I_2''$, at E'_1 true price of bundle X will increase, showing health, and environmental costs, but as we run out of the fuel. This will lower the consumers' income, and it will rearrange the production and redeployment of resources at a different production possibility frontier, shown by income (budget) line $I_1 I_1'$. This shows a major reduction in consumption of X. Consumers will soon recognize benefit of reduction in purchasing X in larger amount of Y they can consume instead. The substitutions of Y for more costly X at E1, is called the substitution effect.

This yet again reflect different technologies and resource allocation the positive externalities or consumers' benefits are measured by $I_1 E_1 I_2$ and their negative externalities from the change will be equal to $I_1' E_1 I_2'$, the loss related to increasing price of X. In a sustainable development model, a large injection of income, more education, and retraining will be needed to entice another shifts to using more of Y bundle. At the new budget line $I_3 I_3'$, at E_4 the consumers will be better off. However, in a developing economy this may prove to be more of a complex proposition than it is proposed on our campuses or political halls, if it even is discussed anymore.

Therefore, in most cases, we adopt technologies to arrive at E_4' for sustainable economic developments. While, we really need to plan to be at E_4, that is wasting much less of diminishing resources. This results in some very peculiar non-market notions as well. One is that cheaper or subsidized fossil fuel is just beneficial to sustainable advancements of economies. Ignoring efficiencies that market price will generate, or negative externalities, which a true price can modify. If a free car was given to every human on earth will that strictly, benefit humanity. If every village had a coal factory, will the globe survive that benefit? The fallacy of composition is not too hard to grasp, but it will not always survive the stronger notion of private gains associated with the needs and wants of services and goods of the markets.

The temporary discourses from the Pareto optimal allocations and economic welfare equilibriums alone can be difficult to overcome. Gather all random Nash-disequilibrium you wish, you will not add them up to a Pareto Optimum Equilibrium Stable system. The ample application of Keynes and monetarism propositions were fought past the 1929 business cycle, until the conservatism of Hover-ism, (a peculiarly implied market notion: we broke it, but will not do anything to fix it because it will eventually fix itself) was circumvented during Roosevelt presidency and the World War Two expenditures and reallocation of purchasing powers.

In such an economic reality, even those with wealth get hurt in an economic depression, and cheap labor is meaningless to all producers, when no one will buy the products. The first proposition is often totally ignored, or fought as redistribution of income. Often, the very people who were helped by it in their mixed economic strategies called it a socialists' notion.

It is not without cause that it is hypothesized here, that perfectly free market economies are chronically deflationary, because they tend not to be perfect, nor always free, nor the legal and political institutions understand the damage they can do to structure as they accumulate rules or centralize power, eroding the same systems. Nor do they understand the problem of wealth-concentration versus wealth creation and the significant each play in the economy.

It is a matter of life and facts that most developing economies do not have the socio-political infrastructure commonly taken for granted in the advanced economies. Moreover, moving from one phase to another creates great taxing on fragile systems, and requires not only newer appropriate technologies but also means to adopt and improve the technologies dealing with bottlenecks as they are formed in the process. These are facts reflected in the major injection of income, as budget line shows in the graph.

Sustainable strategies for economic growth or development can successfully be formulated. Sustainable growth and development strategies are not mutually very exclusive, and they are not independent-theories, they reflect the economies around them.[4] They are not definitely, one time money injection in an economy. That is the most common mistake, which is made regularly. Figure 5 shows dynamic welfare function and set theory and different technologies. It also reflects the need for food, medicine, the minimum infrastructure required, before any

We have accumulated a long list of unfortunate private and governmental attempts to transpose development models, mostly along a projected line towards E_4' in less developing economies. While even gradual and segmental movements toward adaptations of more technologies, which are appropriate, and they are improved production processes will prove more beneficial in the end, when such adjustments can be made. Figure 5 shows the societal utility of productions and consumption (S = D) frontiers, sum of all hypothetical Pareto possible solutions society chooses from bundles x and y combination possible. All productions and Pareto optimal allocations of economic activities of supplies and demands fall within the three sets of societal utilities and production frontiers.

Naturally, all productions possible [for the time span] with all technologies will fall within this sets. Social welfare indifference curves reflect choices and satisfaction possible such that there are sets of points, which are preferred and do benefit the global well-beings, and meet minimum required limits for the survival of bio-diversity versus and Figure 5. Dynamic welfare function and set theory and different technologies resource limitations.

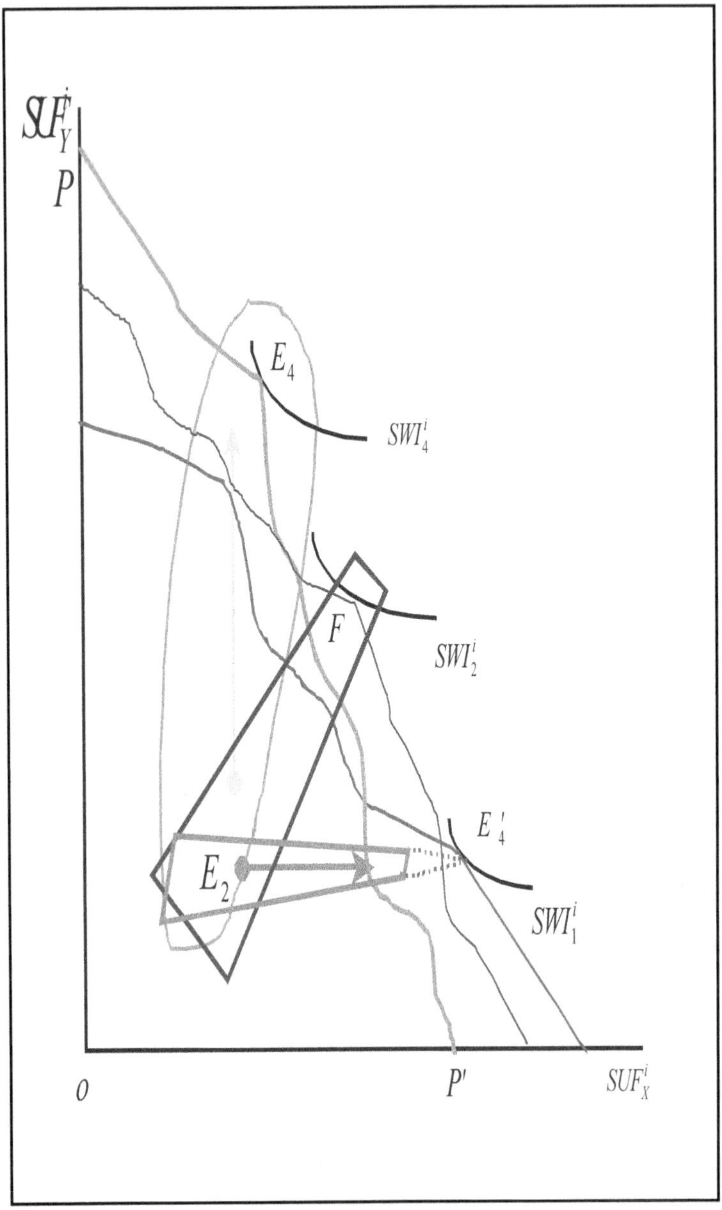

Figure 5. Dynamic welfare function and set theory, and technologies limitations.

However we cannot represent this as unique solution points, because we are studying societal norms, individual Pareto Optimal points of satisfaction fall on or within the bounded sets of numbers in the graph, in a way that they are not worst off without benefits or excluded without sound legal cause or reason, to do otherwise is often to cause harm.

It is at E4, which more of appropriate technological advancements and sustainable progress, and higher and improved satisfaction exists using more of Y bundles of goods and services. These are produced using better appropriate technologies, with optimum employment and income to justify and meet such prices. Either movement from E2 will be a considered an improvement.

However, the resource limitation and population explosion constraints show in the narrowing of the sets in the later period. However, at E4 we have a higher indifference curve and possibility for sustainable progress, even with globally active economies. The economic welfare production-possibility frontiers reflect different technologies and periods.

Notes

[1] These smaller entities comprise large portions of developing economies.

[2] Fracing technology has been around. Recently its use in natural gas and oil exploration has expanded exponentially. It has coupled with directional drilling. Without appropriate laws, small landowners do not have the knowledge or a chance to confront abuse, until it shows up in cancer or other ailments of the livestock or family members.

[3] The mathematical presentation for the third lemma, sustainability has been introduced in Teconomic boom.

[4] This is possible as included in Dr. Bahman Fakhraie multi-variables production function.

CHAPTER 4

TECHNOLOGIES, WELFARE THEORY STRATEGIES, IMPLICATIONS

The addition of a new road to a village is a new technological infrastructure, which brings stream of new benefits to an area over time. Adjacent businesses, which want to trade in bulk, can do so with ease, and less costs per quantity.

Cost Benefit of Technology and Supply Expansions

A conversion dirt road to larger payment road, which expand trade and traffic and increases commerce as the result, access to health care and urban medical benefit can also further expand the benefits. At least, the increase in the traffic is measureable.

Figure 6 shows the added benefits from utilizing new infrastructure.

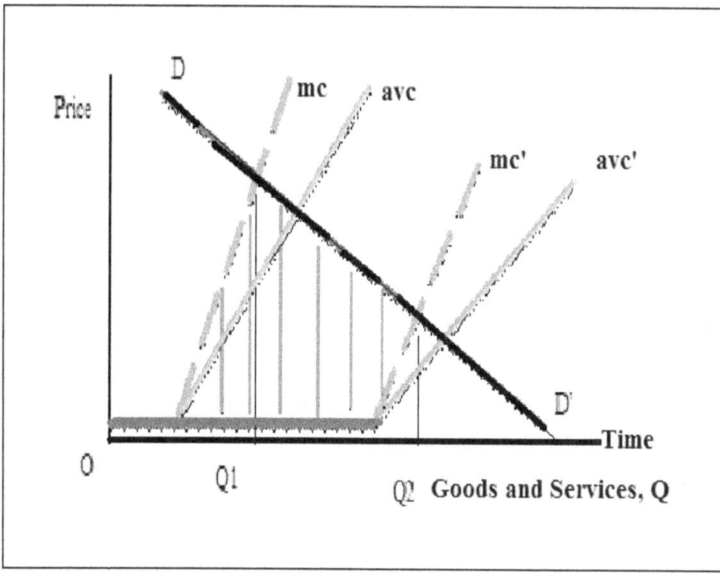

Figure 6. Benefits from new infrastructure.

The benefit increase is the shaded area under the demand curve and marginal costs. It is not considered as an increase in welfare of the village, unless the real income partly or in aggregate increases, without harming the real income of other people in the village.

Producer Surplus

Total cost of all variables used in production of quantity Q, are the values under the curve identified by OSDQ.

The curve is supply curve, which is the marginal cost curve of production function. In case of perfect competition condition, the profit can go the zero, while rent or producer surplus is greater than zero.[1] In figure 7, producers' surplus is shown by SCD. This goes to the suppliers of the firms' productive variables.

Nevertheless, in cases of monopsony, oligopoly, and imperfect competitions prices may over shoot the average costs substantially. While these technologies, regulatory, or regional cases of monopsony will serves to motivate entrepreneurial spirits, and productive risk taking, targeted investment, it can become recursive in debilitating aggregate demand.

Therefore, the matters of redistributive macro policies are consequentially important, in balancing the forces of the economy. So that demand and supply become accommodating to growth of the economy in a sustainable manner. These have been experienced historically in industrialization of the western economies, in auto and energy industries. In modern time, technology-industries, the computer, and robotic related industries will face this as well.

Figure 7 shows producer's surplus or rent. That is, the SCD portion, per each unit Q. D, is when the demand curve meets the average cost curve of the producers.

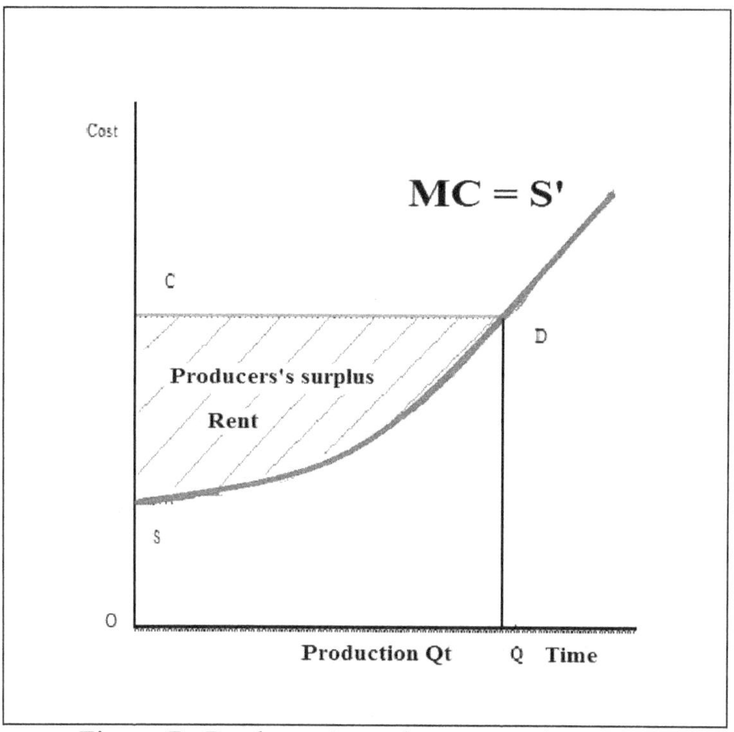

Figure 7. Producers' surplus, or rent in perfect competition.

Figure 8 shows the increase in the producers' surplus after the injection of technologies has shifted the supply curve outward. The area designated as D1D2S', shows the difference, and the increase in the producer's surplus, after a technological change has shifted the supply curve. The price remains the same by assumption.

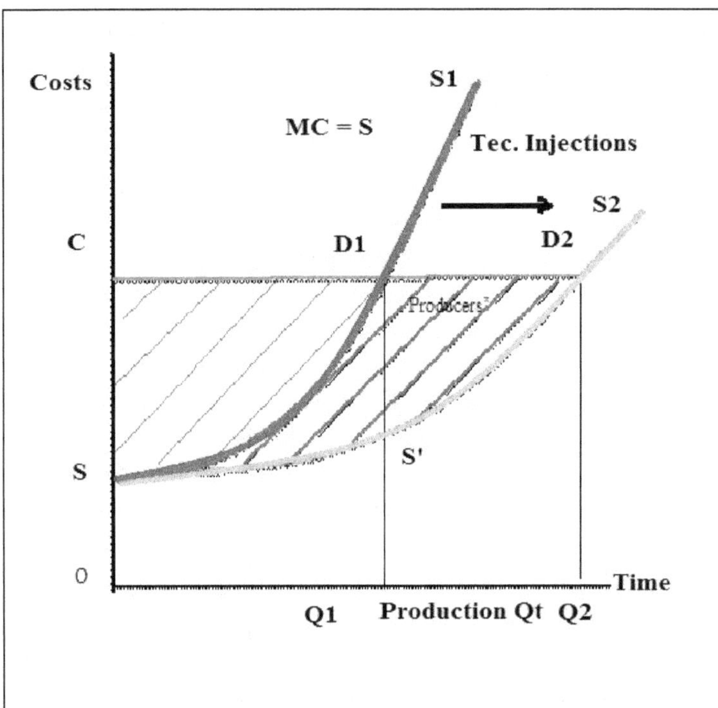

Figure 8. Producers' surplus, technology injection, and supply curve.

The alterations of certain conditions influence the ceteri paribus and the market conditions, therefore, the arithmetic of benefit calculation in the economy. When a technological injection expands the supply curve outward, the consumer can afford to buy more of the same good or service at the lower price. The consumer surplus increases by amount of the present larger surplus less the previous amount of nominal surplus.

Figure 9 shows producer's surplus increase due to technological injects, and supply expansion. The graph shows the effect of such technological injection. In addition, S1S2P' is this producer surplus under the demand curve. It is the nature of market, that supply and demand reduces that area. A notion, which seems to have become unpalatable to some modern political parties.

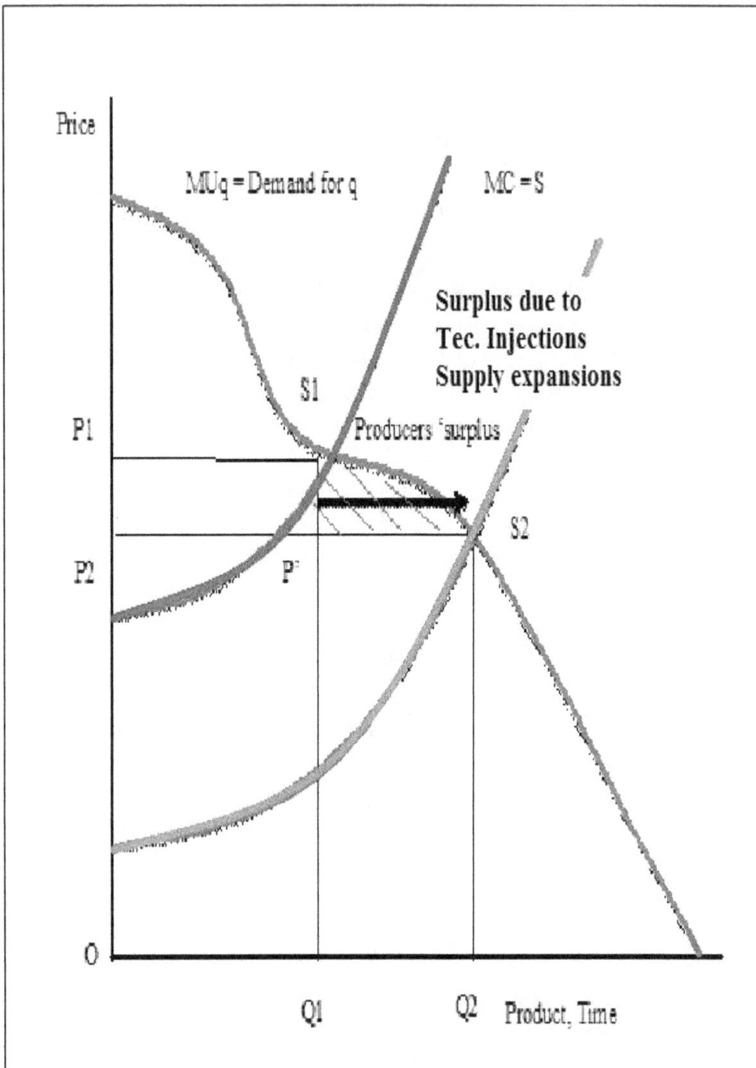

Figure 9. Producer's surplus increase due to tec-injects and supply expansion.

Consumer Surplus

Consumers and producers that come into the market place gain an additional degree of satisfaction per each additional unit they buy or sell, until the value of the additional unit drops to null. That is the last unit traded. The accumulation of these added benefits are titled consumer and producer surpluses, which is measured.

When marginal utility of each item consumed equals, the marginal cost of the production of each unit, goods and services prices, consumer purchases the most possible basket of goods and services, subject to his or her budgetary constraints.[2] What the consumer purchase has a nominal price and shadow value to the consumer above the market price that is the nominal worth of individual consumer surplus for each purchase.

That odd item, a golf club at the garage sale sold for $10, while the buyer thinks it was $80 at the sport outlets, just last week. Therefore, the consumer buys it feeling it was a good buy. The rare painting of dead western artist of "bovine roping," sold at $50 at the church rummage sale, consumer buys it, because it looks good. The buyers googled it (look it up on the internet), and then took it down to the local dealer, he was told the value was $50,000 or more at a real auction! The arbitrages $40 for the golf club, and $50,000 less expenses, are the consumers' surpluses.

The consumer obviously cannot measure the astatic of the painting, but he or she can measure consumer surplus nominal index. The former example is not sufficient to increase the real income; however, in the latter example the real income will be much higher after the sale. Therefore, the welfare of at least the seller will have increased substantially.

All those people seen at garage sales are there under the dictate of consumer surplus economic model, even if they did not know it. They seek the largest arbitrages, they can find, if they understood they are there to increase their consumers' surpluses. Total revenue spend on the q is shown by OPD'Q. The demand curve is constructed under certain assumptions. Perfect competition and ceteris paribus as we have studied it are complex assumptive construct to uphold. It does help to understand what they are.

These assumptions are perfect knowledge of market participants, population size, tastes, prices of all other goods and services, given incomes, nominal or real, thus distribution issues. The changes can alter elasticity and shapes of demand and supply curve, thus the benefit estimations.[3] While we use equalities rather than equations, there is a need for cautious analytical comprehensions.

The demand curve is downward sloping; therefore, it is not a case of Geffin good. The money income is assumed constant. In this specific case, a reduction in price of his consumption good increases the benefit to that consumer. It has the same effect as rise in the real income, thus it is an increase in the consumer welfare. Total utility of q versus how much the consumer pays for it, constitute consumer surplus.[4] The utility and consumer surplus serves as the motivators for sustained demand, for technological injections in the economy. That could also motivate consumers to seek higher wages, income in more urban areas (mobility of workers) in developing world, and immigration results in larger issues.[5]

Figure 10 shows consumer surplus from utilizing each additional product q. Consumer surplus is shown by DD'P.[6] That is for one consumer one technological item; however, in aggregate they will become substantial, and influence the sustainability of demand for technological items.

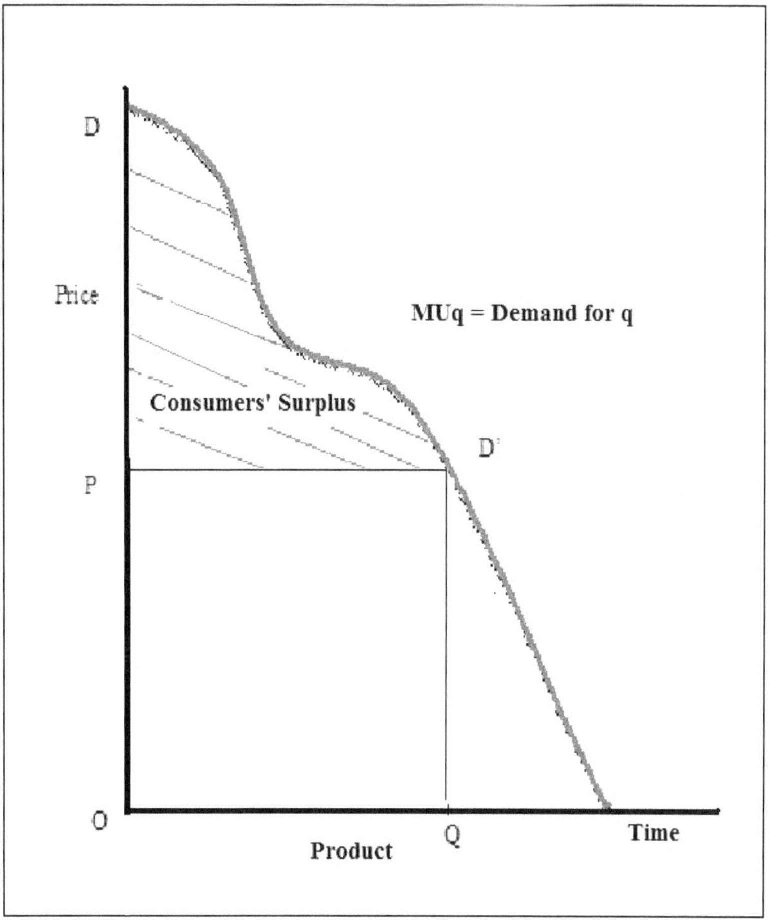

Figure 10. Consumer surplus in utilizing each additional product q.

Figure 11 shows the shorter-term effect of technologic injection and the related price adjustment. The consumer surplus increase is shown by PDD'P'. Figure 12 shows consumers' surplus increase due to technological injects and demand shift. Figure 12 shows the effect of technological injection, which has expanded the demand outward.

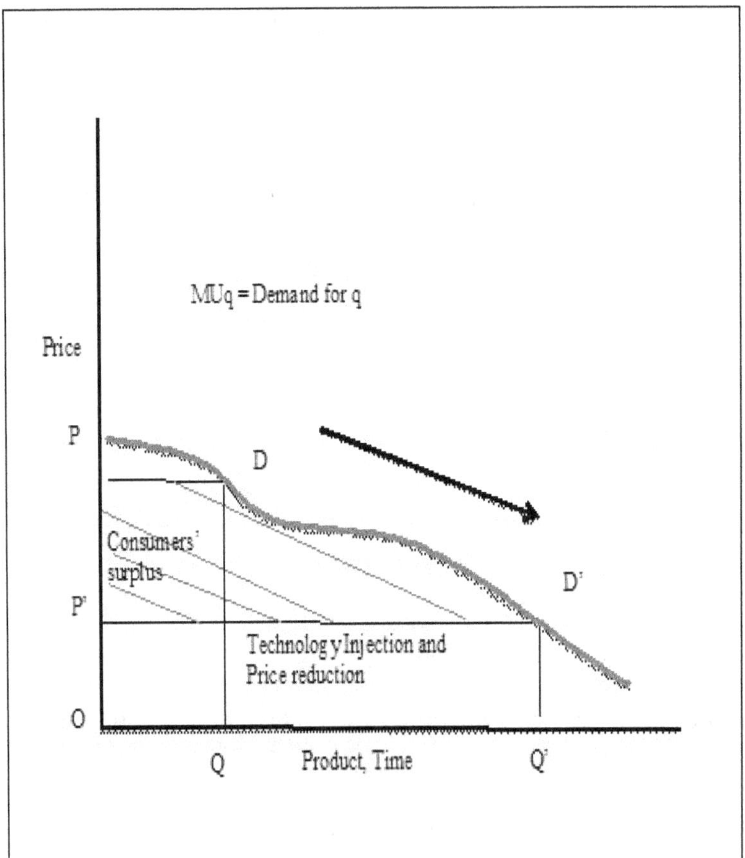

Figure 11. Consumer surplus from utilizing each additional product q.

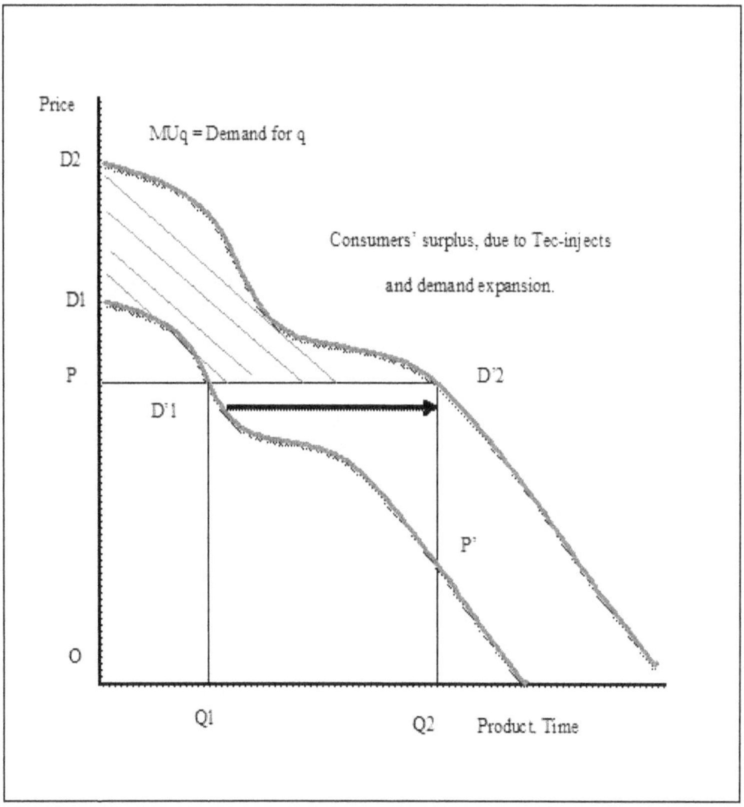

Figure 12. Consumers' surplus increase due to tec-injects and demand shift.

Figure 12 shows the effect of technological injection, which has expanded the demand outward, prices, and nominal income staying the same ceteris paribus, D1D2D'2D'1 shows the consumer surplus increases due to the technological injection. The technical advancement leads to expansion of curves, the downward sloping demand curve, and the positively sloping supply curve. In order to measure the consumer and producer's surpluses, the price is assumed constant. Figure 13, Surpluses increase due to Technological injection, which expands demand and supply curve outward. Consumer surplus difference is shown as SS'1D'2. The producer surplus is identified by S1D'2D'.

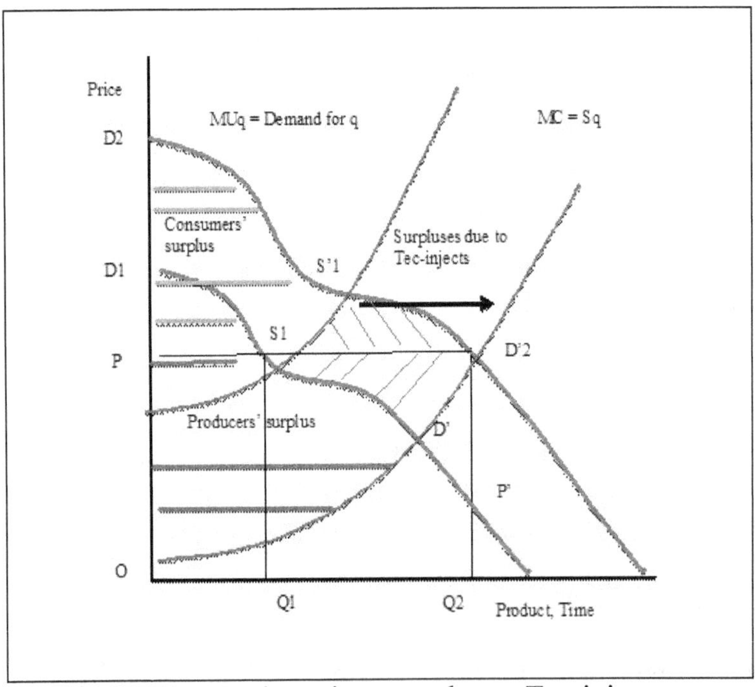

Figure 13. Surpluses increase due to Tec-injects.

The Distribution Theory Implication

The policy implication of limited resource allocation, requires distribution of limited variables as inputs to production of commodities goods and services (including technologies), and distribution of goods and services among various the consumers, and the maintenance of economic functionality on a slight growth path determines the sustainability of a productive and developing economy.

Optimization in Microeconomic and welfare theory of economics means the operational maximization of resource or produce uses in satisfaction of consumer utility function.[7] That is, in Pareto optimality formulation we will find marginal utility ratios of goods and services equals their prices, and costs ratios.[8]

The producers' profit function is set for maximization subject to the variable cost of wages, salaries, and rents.

The marginal product ratios of variables are equal to the ratio of wages, rents, and wages of variables.

In recent political history, redistribution, socialism, and other issues, have been utilized to cloud and confuse the proper importance of distribution theory, as a necessity economic machinery of any functional market economic theory. This is for the following reasons. One is, it maintains a broken political economic model to keep taxes lower, than functionally possible in a macroeconomics of market oscillations in a market economy. Two is, the dishonest placement of institutionally fixed arrangement to set pay packages higher, in the cooperate-executive markets. Three, a most perverse new political tool to break social, governmental, and cooperation contracts after, in order to deny workers their portion of pay-packages in their retirements. This is yet another criminally insane idea to underpay variables bellow their equilibrium wages.[9] It is an unhelpful backward move to the Marxian maxim, which called this method of under subsistence pay in microeconomic capital production market as a brutal method. John Bates Clark concluded his economic theory of distribution from marginal productivity theory of distribution.[10] Clark could have not had these levels of abuses and machinations in mind. The negative externalities implied are too large to be ignored.

In modern economies, when we here about free market, the assumptive foundations are about perfect competition in the free market economies. However, when it comes to redistribution in modern economies, the vandalized discussions only parrot the assumptive foundations, but they are monopolistic or institutionally are twisted to enrich the very few. They falsify the indices to look like everyone is properly employed, productive, and benefiting from proper distributions of wealth. However, the decaying disposable real income of the population presents the ultimate facts and proofs.

In that light, the growing deficits are theft of public wealth to enrich the few, a perverse wealth concentration models that has brought many market economies ruination. The socialization of risks and costs, and the privatization and wealth-concentration of beneficial profits are not perfect market solutions, and functional market capitalism. That is not only a road to serfdom, but also a high way to predation. The best title for it is a monopolistic, imperfect road to unsustainable market capitalism.

A perfect example is 1920s, and 1930s United State pre-depression economic machinations, and the refined but dishonest verbiages about the gliders and bling of triumphalism predating the prolonged disastrous results. It is astonishing how political organizational culture has also ventured off the democratic path, which parallel perfect competition, when voters and not the moneyed-interests are represented in a collective bargaining settlement of values.

Small deviations from perfect competition at micro level yields to improper distribution in market place. In aggregation and at macro level, especially in the age of mega corporations and multinationals magnified by technological injections, there are distributional misadventures, which would yield to unsustainability conditions, stated with comfortable degree of certainty.[11] Author studies the macroeconomics case, and the injection of corrective measures is a technological injection.[12] In the market economies, which are consumer demand driven economies, there are profound influence in form of prolonged negative oscillations of the economy.[13] For example, the use of real disposable income over time will show if economic welfare has increased, decayed, or remained flat. In same time, the surpluses and the positive externalities have taken place. The impacts are the underperformance, and unemployment due to such insufficient and improper distribution of national wealth.

Dynamic Social Welfare Theories and technologies

A systematic analysis using set theory eases the comprehension of otherwise complex abstract hypotheses that unfold over a long time span.

Figure 14 shows dynamic social welfare utilities of different technological solutions. The basic economic assumptions are not abandoned. The higher utility is preferred to lower utility, welfare frontiers are first reflect at the outset of the same period frontiers, but in the final graph a frontier TT' is uses to show long term social welfare frontier enveloping the out extreme of intertemporal social welfare frontiers and multi-periodical utilities [at t_0, t_1] as indifference curves [SWI]. Each bounded set shown as [E or F] reflect series of points, which mean more than, the Pareto Optimum locus of individuals'

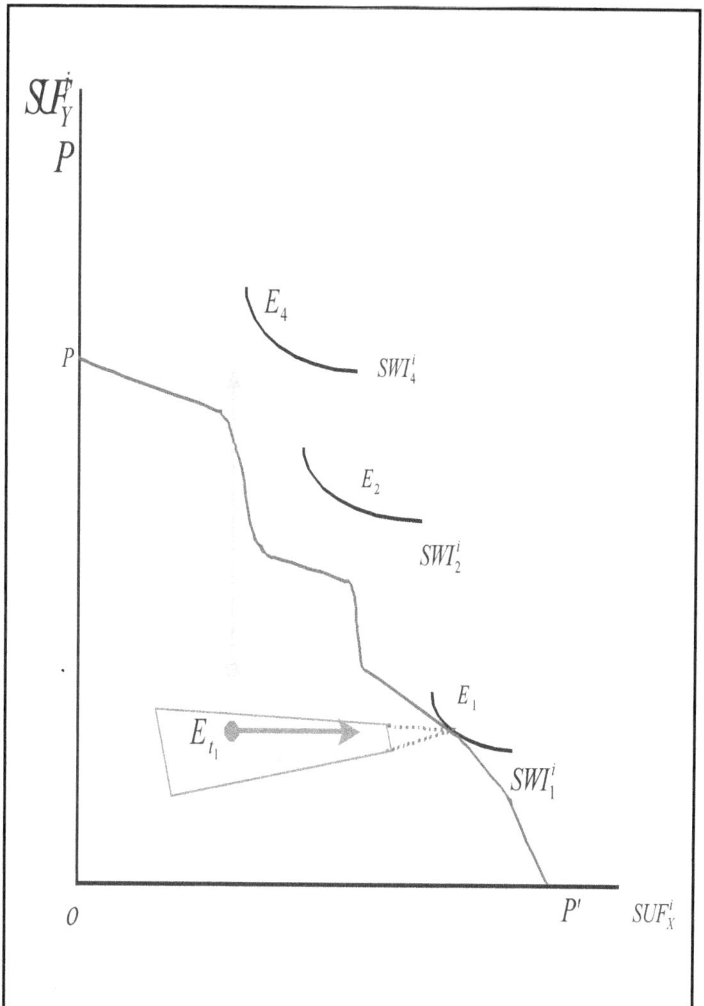

Figure 14. Dynamic social welfare utilities of different technological solutions.

satisfactions at different levels within the set, reflecting decisions on appropriate technologies, pricing and even new look at governance, which would leave resources for future economic activities. The first graph reflects the limitation of technology duplications even if these are pollution causing problematic technologies and strategies, which would strip resources and renders urban centers too toxic for normal life. Therefore, to meet some future periods it will fall short of global economic needs.

The bounded set includes more than the Pareto Optimum locus of individuals' satisfactions at different levels within the set, leaving resources for future economic activities. However, These requires less consumptive extensive level of living, and generally less market imperfections and more true costs (externalities linked prices), than at this bounded set. The bounded set does not narrow but either stays the same longer, or expand over time, reflecting the intertemporal investments in appropriate technologies and increasing consumer Pareto Optimum and preferred satisfactions in the future by diversifications of resources and prolonging the usage of diminishing resources. This in the set also shows initial effects of limited corrective actions in the market place, but reality reflecting market true conditions and narrowing of the set start as pressure on limited resources shows. This strategy may prolong economic life to last, but not as long as the best strategy.

The narrowing bounded set at E_1 reflect even more of the market imperfections and imperfection of democracies, which stifle rights to ownership, entrepreneurship, and right to vote or test opinions, specially concerning wastefulness of diminishing resources. Examples for economic activities were ubiquitous up to the early part of last millennium. However, vivid examples of late 1800s United Kingdoms' pollution after steam engine led to more industrial production, later in United States metal mining and steal production had the same impact on East Costs. The general understanding assumes that it is very difficult to set conditions or systems to satisfy humanity in totality, however, satisfying the most such that (x > y > z) for example [80%>60%>40%] with harming the least in the reverse order seems to be the best conditions we can assume at this time. More free competitive markets, and relative free trades, and free mobility's of capital and workers, a rational currency exchange mechanism will do a lot to minimize harm, where rational beings may exchange their differences rather than engage in conflicts. Each failure, knowingly or otherwise, waste resources, replaces functional systems and reduce trusts in any further attempts to correct fundamental short comings present or transferred to a region.

Alas, the horrendously poor circumstances and Dickensian inhuman conditions around Asia, Africa, South America (granted that positive examples like South Africa also exists) and elsewhere invites the need for ideas to improve level of living globally. Simply going back to military models of last millenniums will prove to be the most destructive and mutually resource wasting of all options. Even employing the most constructive of the militarists' solution, the Marshal plan, with the old technologies, without thought provoking selections among appropriate modern technologies can be very limiting. However, with appropriate commitments globally to remedy mistakes and make proactive corrective fall back positions transfer of appropriate technologies with education and skills transfers, job creation and sustainable development will resume and much of current ills will very slowly start on an constructive growth pass. Figure 15 shows dynamic social welfare utility and frontier of different technologies, the bounded set E_2 reflect more correct selections of technologies, and a constructive path, with reliance on integrated production and smaller more efficient and less polluting production units. Figure 16 shows dynamic social welfare utilities of optimum technological solutions.

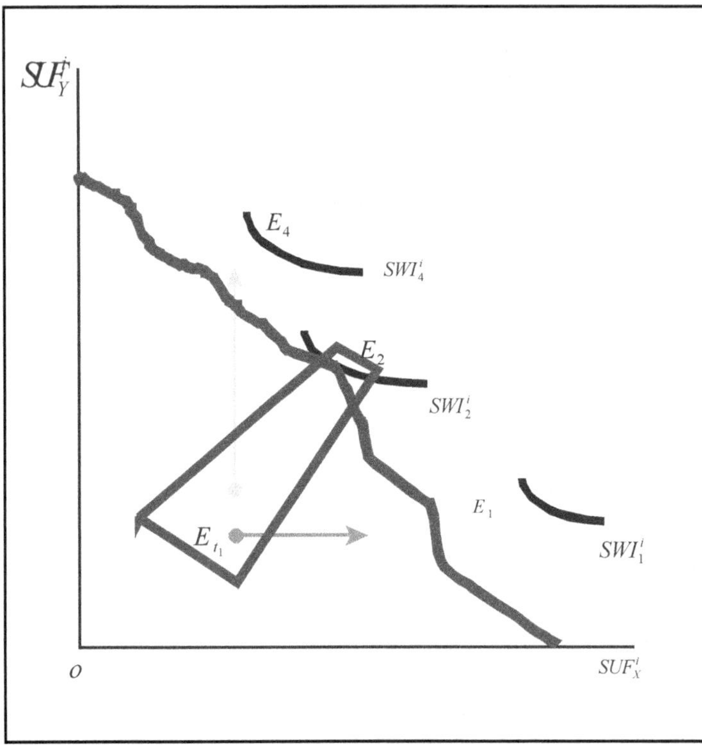

Figure 15. Dynamic social welfare utility and frontier of different technologies.

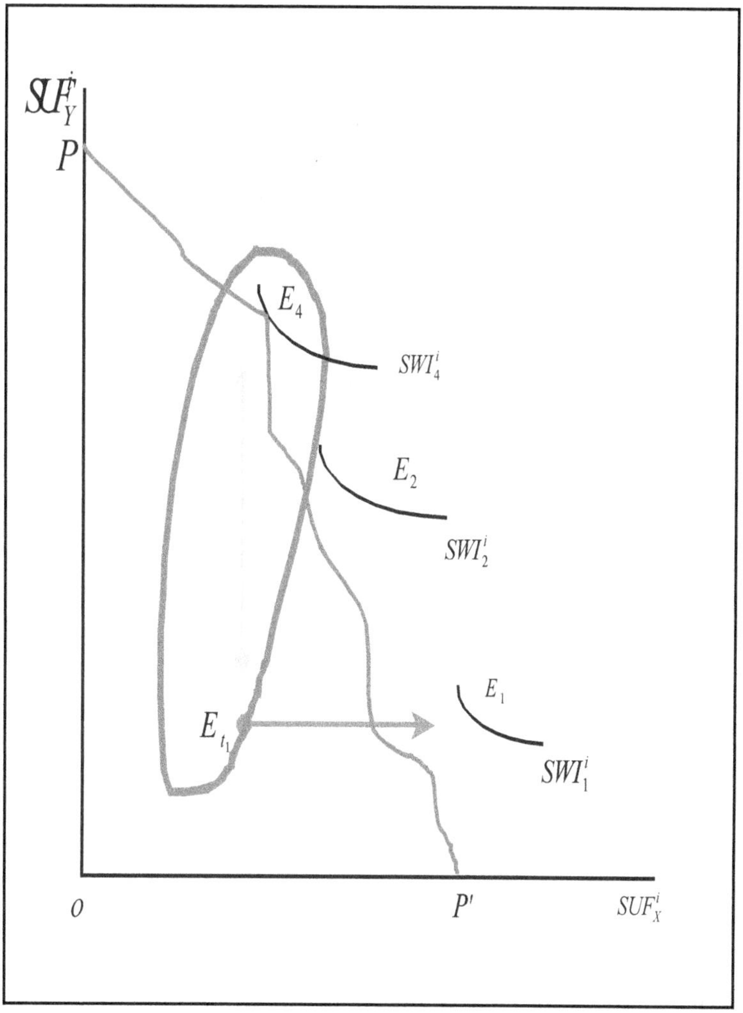

Figure 16. Dynamic social welfare utilities of optimum technological solutions.

Resources become more available as pricing reduces wasteful over the social welfare frontier level and utility are higher than under previous graph. The true comprehension of science, sometime come with the dramatic drawing in the reality of scientific events, which for some inexplicit reason remain hidden to most for an uncertain periods ..

The last graph figure 16 becomes clearer as we see difference in level of lives over long periods My own life experience was growing dualism of urban, rural life in a developing world in 1960s, where technological advancement was slowly crawling their way into our city lives. The rural lives within 20 miles would only see the same modernity but at a later date and much slower rate. People would live and die with new medicine and live with more relative comfort when electrical washing machines and tractors showed up. The down side of development also left death-marks around, as well. More universally known example, is the black toxic pollution clouds common to London industry in 1800s, now they are known as brown urban industry clouds globally. However, the population of the world has exploded exponentially, since the Malthusian dilemma was published.

The varieties of industries have evolved to employ far wider number of people, some do not use coal, some use less energy than others do, and some cause no pollution at all. One more example perhaps was the public television attempt to take modern families out of the city and put them in rural life minus electrical and modern technologies.

Figure 16 shows dynamic social welfare utilities of different technological solutions, using a bounded set. Experiencing the technological gap can readily see the converted bounded set of possibilities available to present population versus early 1900s, or 1800s. Therefore, given such technological possibilities exist or researched for the future, we can see it is not such a leap of academic judgment.

The bounded set E_4 present such a scenario, where technological progress allows for more population live in global wealth with much reduces waste extensive and less energy using methodologies. The perfection of market allows for true costs of resources to let sustainable growth and development in these economies. The improvements will allow economies to afford a more comfortable level of living, without limiting resources for the future. The current population expansions require more innovative scholarships to find the sustainable development comfort zones.

The bounded set F_{t_2} includes the Pareto Optimum locus of individuals' satisfactions at different levels within the set, leaving resources for different economic activities. The three different technological regimes are for different set of technologies. This set contain three different technological options used in an aggregate global economy, the least favored options uses the most resources, produces large direct waste, and pollution as indirect waste, direct costs, and indirect costs related to pollution and social costs, which are ignored in the short term accountings to fund the system.

Another illustration would be the co-existence of an electronic software industry, next to a manufacturing production unit, next to a rural small farm region. Other more complicated example would the integrated auto-production, with tires made in Mexico, electronics in Japan, interior material in Iran, engine in USA, and the auto can be assembled in different regions like China, or Canada, or Europe. Figure 17 shows a global overview of the dynamic social welfare utilities of different technological solutions.

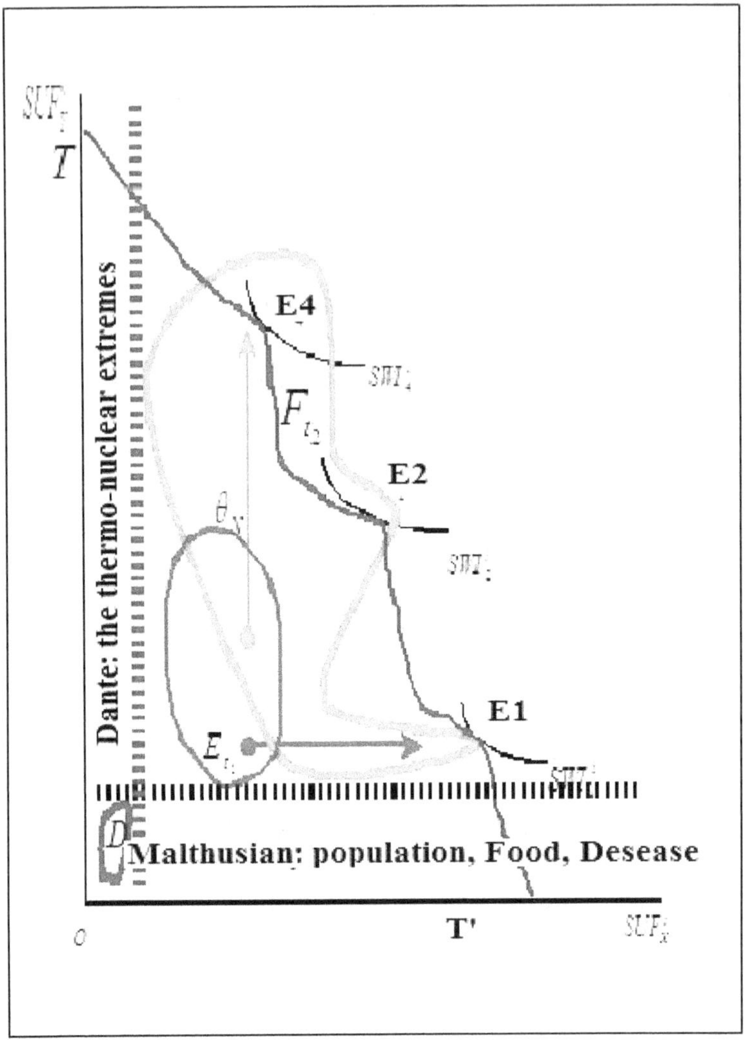

Figure 17. Dynamic social welfare utilities of different technolo**gi**cal solutions.

That is the sustainability lemma that passed, for mathematical presentation of Sheppard lemma and Lagrange formulations refer to appendix, A. Some elements of this example already exists in the real world, however, greater application run into geopolitics and obsolete technologies of the last millenniums. Some application exists, because without it, the current population could not have been sustained, and global disaffection, famine, disease, wars, as much as they have been unrelenting, they would have been much worst. It is in neglecting these conditions, which humanity invites more of them in the future. This model allow for the bio-diversity, cultural uniqueness and production methodologies that encourages diverse production solution to culturally distinct groups, with limitation regarding technological by-products and waste, which are too lethal to global biology.

The following set theory formulation states some of the assumptions involved in the above graphs:

This would deal with the as serious limitation and the fallacy of composition that we have been operating with, as soon as technological duplication becomes our only means development. Another serious limitation would be new technologies in terms of exchange regimes accommodating neutral transactions and some globally and politically justified circumstances.

$$F \neq \{\varnothing\}; F \approx \left\{\left\{E_1\right\} \cup \left\{E_2\right\} \cup \left\{E_4\right\}\right\}$$

$$\ni \left\{E_4\right\} \rangle \left\{E_2\right\} \rangle \left\{E_1\right\} \,\&\, \left\{F_{t_2}\right\} \rangle \left\{E_{t_1}\right\}$$

Therefore, a modern global economy integrated and diversified, which yields the economic welfare production frontier TT', which can meet different indifference curves is possible. This approach is preferred to the duplication of more constraining technologies for development.

The bounded set E4, includes more than the Pareto Optimum locus of individuals' satisfactions at different levels within the set, leaving resources for future economic activities. However, These requires less consumptive extensive level of living, and generally less market imperfections and more true costs (externalities reflecting prices), than at other bounded sets. The bounded set does not narrow but either stays the same longer, or expand over time, reflecting the intertemporal investments in appropriate technologies and increasing consumer Pareto Optimum and preferred satisfactions in the future by diversifications of resources and prolonging the usage of diminishing resources(by the maximization of set {F}). This also shows initial effects of limited corrective actions in the market place, but reality reflecting market true conditions and narrowing of the set start as pressure on limited resources shows.

The benefit of non-military appropriate technological advancements will become clear (minimization of set {D} subject to its constraints), when they make possible a production possibility frontier reflecting the new transformed economies [TT'], which allow for adaptations without triggering the fallacy of composition current models trigger. Most current models by duplicating advanced economies' discarded energy-use- intensive technologies will trigger very limiting options in the shorter run, the exponential increases in the brown industrial plums, Ozone problems, waste issues, nuclear wastes, water toxins, and fish kills, in and around urban centers globally, are not sometimes in the future.

There are actual hopeful signs. When skipping certain technologies a generation for more efficient ones, like the wired phones for new digital-cell phones, or use of propane instead of wood or coal or oil fuels are adopted readily in a larger segment of the global households not knowing the extend of technologies in an actual advanced economies' households. In the rural centers the uses of village stationed- propane cookers, shifts non-heating fuel (energy) uses substantially. However, introductions of cars and personal transformations will quickly push more communities into the brown clouds.

The other wonderful modern technology of communication may yet have other surprises for us. For a long time, the world looked at the implosions of Soviet system, not understanding how communication made comparatives realities so unbearable. The world suddenly could vote by their eyes, legs, and opinions, a democracy without party systems affiliations and overt media manipulation and political-sausage making that goes with it. We will revisit this phenomenon again in business cycles, capital concentration, income and wage package economic distortions, and human capital motilities globally, until we can grasp its true significance.

A realistic study of global economic conditions leaves very few choices away from constructive and cooperative endeavors, however non-passive it gets, toward minimization of conflicts for better cooperation for improved economic employment of resources, human and non-human capital, and shared functioning economies on shrinking productive soil. At times, when humanity is not on one of the many destructive side roads, we are optimistically closer to the true constructive path. Let us hope we get on it before it is too late!

What Is In It For The Real World

It is clear that advanced economies cannot deliver a dream life to more than 5 percent of their populations, while the middle class level of living and numbers have been re-modified and have been shrinking over times, as the last two decades of anti-immigrations rhetorical verbiage and laws, however unconstructive, show these concerns in most advanced economies. The hope for a functional lifestyle for growing populations depends on hopeful ways to study the resource uses of this millennium. It is also more clear that corruption of governance cannot be blamed for all evils, but Enronism and the market-disconnects, become dangerously implosive or worst dust devils in smaller economies.

Despite the noise, in reality larger economies are not protected against it, either. Beyond health, education, defense, and regulatory duties, it is left to mostly private economic mechanisms, processes to formulated future life, by designs of new and appropriate non-military technologies for best limited-resource uses and wealth creation, for the level of life and diversities of lives, which would be accommodating to cultural diversities without extensive conflict creations. For the most part, this increasingly falls on the smaller units of productions, while the larger units modify the laws in their own self-interest, under condition harmful to the wellbeing of all.

In addition, increasingly these smaller production units are immigrants as well as native risk takers. This experiments help grasp the abstracts. The three-container small-scale experiment easily shows you that three containers have more volume separately, than when they are submerged into each other. Keep that in mind when you hear the next austerity plan, which will keep income and demand down, make unemployed thousands of teachers, postal workers, and house builders, government and none government workers, in order to transfer tax-break revenue to the top one percent of the population, mega global cooperation, and too big to fail banks. Only balanced approaches will work.

Figure 18, bucket experiments, and budget austerity plans shows proper uses of technological injections in the economy increases chances for more employment and economic growth. Figure 19 shows the bucket experiment, Tec-injections, and job growth.

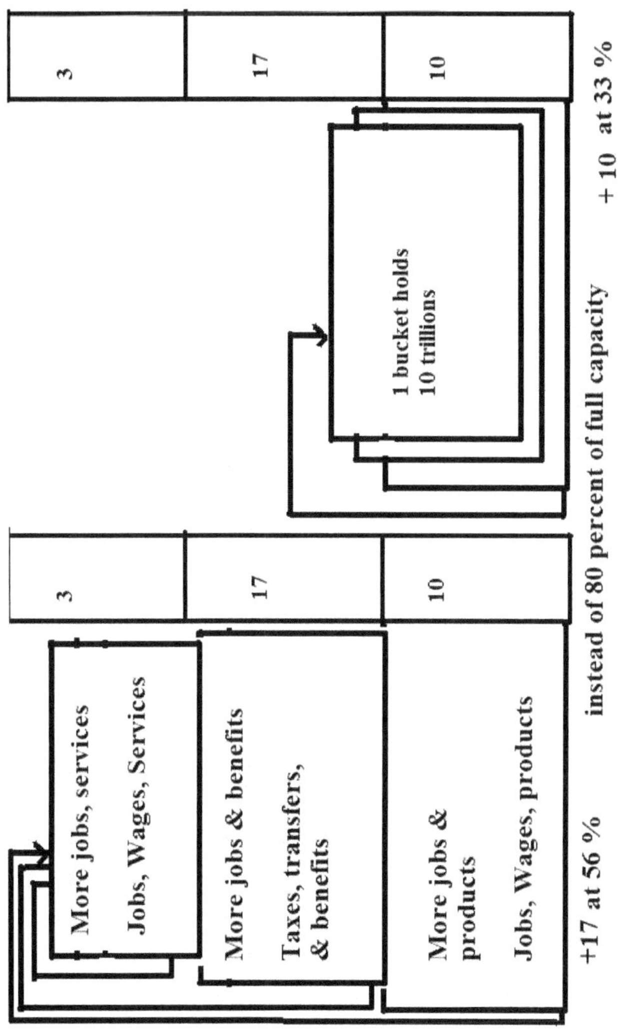

Figure 18. The bucket experiments and the budget austerity plans.

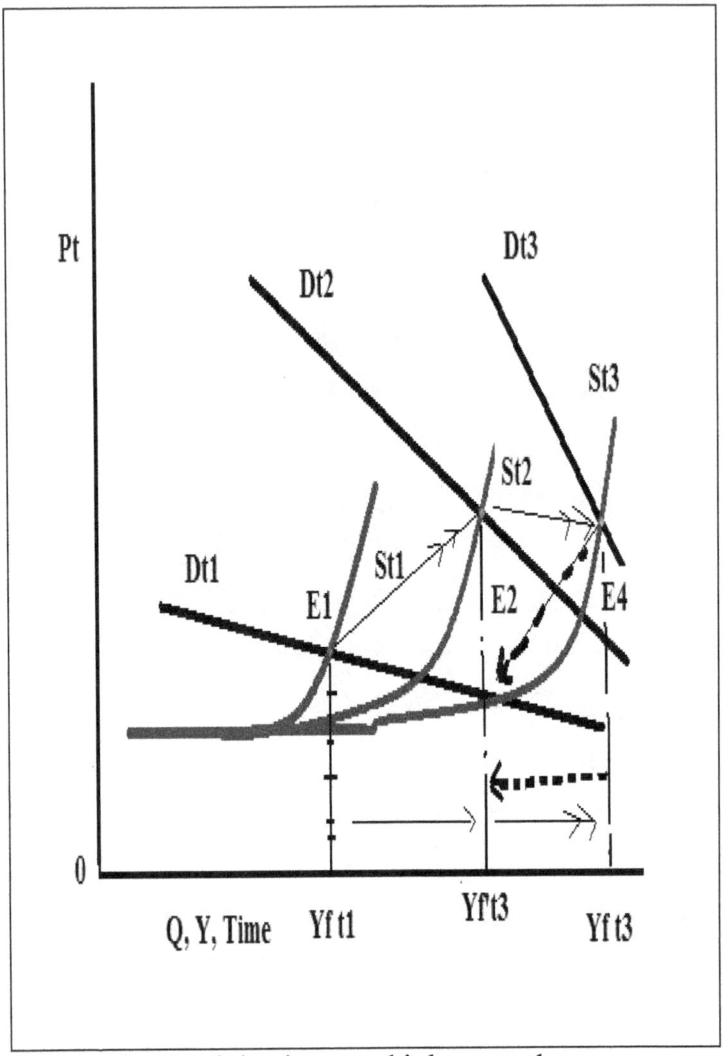

Figure 19. Tec-injections, and jobs growth.

The shift in aggregate demands with technological injections of the supply curve will increase gross national product, and full employment ratios. That is deficits are important remedy tool, if invested wisely in domestic economy for counter cyclical causes, and increase in aggregate demands with higher wages and jobs.

Appropriate technologies, diversities, and getting on the right constructive path, accommodate our future life options, so that they do not narrow or diminish, but expand. Example in the more complex, advance, and economically integrated economies, Japan still serves as a good example of massive pro-active transfer of appropriate technologies can achieve. One should note that Japan is very selective about how and what technologies they filter and transfer, and they pro-actively modify technologies for their evolving conditions. Even Japanese are aware that another 100 countries in their image will run out of demand and resources in short order. There are logically powerful tendencies for natural diversities in cultural tastes, and demands, and tolerances globally, thus the logic of diversities in methodologies to supply them.

The economic movements toward free trade in China serve as a good example to study the impact of limited baby steps to adopt relatively free market mechanisms. Democratization has been even more guarded in light of Russian experiences, and some Western relative democracies cultivation of non-democracies. The clear results will perhaps appear early in this millennium, as China meets the challenges of being the second global super power and economic cycles. If successful, given the size of their population, they will attract academic studies.

Smaller scales, uses of propane instead of other fuels, small village stations for cooking, and water pumps have already improved health conditions. Water containing and re-channeling, in more drought regions has also shown good results. However, urban regions, are the sources of polluting, and need to be an important part of the solution. They are also, where the unemployed population is concentrated. Another reason, computer-robotic automation at the expenses of labor wages may prove to be more of a global disaster, which ought to look at compensatory and distributional policy balances.

The global options are limited, not all we desire are distributed justly, or in egalitarian ways, however, with open markets mechanism, democracies, and some infrastructures the level of lives will improve in growing circles of humanity than present situations allows in large regions of Africa, Asia, and South America.

However it is comically insincere, that advanced mixed economies, all beneficiaries of Keynesian redistributions' theories especially in economic down-turns, all become self-prescribed Adam Smith capitalists' economists on behalf of trans-global monopolists (which even Adam Smith would not recognize, or support intellectually), when the issue of North–South or sustainable development and economic growth for South up for discussion.

Unfortunately, the current degree of human miseries and ubiquity of global digitalized multi-media communications are such that we will share the humanities' unemployment, the fortune and misfortunes alike, globally where ever we are, and regardless of any moral ambiguities or theological complexities and differences. Either, we are fueling the flames, which will burn all, or societies resolve our differences and agree to grow the trees and crops of heavens together to feed all?

The concept of national wealth building has expanded here to a global concept of wealth building with careful selection of appropriate technologies to accommodate sustainable strategies. These are different concepts from personal wealth concentration, or wealth accumulation by zero or negative effective tax policy at the expense of social contracts, jobs, infrastructure, commerce, etc. If there are accommodative tax policies, and regulatory modifications, they have to balance the holistic impacts with the cost-benefit trade-offs to create higher average incomes, wages, jobs.

These will assist progress along the integration strategies to improve human conditions globally, to complement Schumpeterian creative-destruction worst microeconomic cases. The dynamic macroeconomic creative-construction strategies associated with technological injections have been the proper emphases of this book. Along with series of new teconomic books, they are to avoid the implications of economic failures of market imperfections policies, and respond to growing the economy constructively, and induce sustainable developments needs of humanity in present time.

§§THE END§§

Notes

[1] William J. Baumol, Economic Theory and Operational Analysis, 4th ed., (New Jersey: Prentice-Hall, 1977),595 [or ibid 595]

[2] This is when an under payment bellow subsistence level, will have a magnified impact on demand and supply, thus on the aggregates of the national and global economy. The ceteris paribus conditions do not apply.

[3] Edward Joshua Mishan, *Cost-Benefit Analysis*, 4th Ed. London: Unwin Hyman, 1988, 55.

[4] William J. Baumol, Economic Theory and Operational Analysis, 4th ed., (New Jersey: Prentice-Hall, 1977),498-499 [or ibid 498-499]

[5] Dr. Fakhraie paper on duality raised the issue of sustainability in developing economy, in light of non-Marxist revolution in Iran, 1970-1980.

[6] William J. Baumol, Economic Theory and Operational Analysis, 4th ed., (New Jersey: Prentice-Hall, 1977), 498-499

[7] Jules Dupuit, uses monetary units to measure consumer 'surplus as the area under the demand curve and the paid price line.
J. Dupuit, "On the Measurement of Utility of Public works," (1844)
K. J. Arrow and T. Scitovsky, eds., *Reading in Welfare Economics, American Economic Association*, Vol. XIII, Homewood Illinois: Richard D. Irwin, Inc., 1969

[8] Vilfredo Pareto, analytical work in constraint maximization to obtain maximum utility of each consumer, without harming another in Pareto optimality.

[9] Kerr ed., *Das Kapita*l, Vol. I, Chapter VI, 189-192.

[10] John Bates Clark, *The Distribution of Wealth*, New York: The Macmillan Company, 1899, 7-8
"the different classes of men <people> who combine their forces in industry have no grievances against each other… <under the perfect competition the distribution> gives every agent of production the amount of wealth which that agent create."

[11] Ibid, 1-2.

[12] Bahman Fakhraie, *Technological Injection, Dynamic New Capital Measurements, and Production Theory in Economics*, (Utah: PhD Dissertation, University of Utah Economics Dept., 2010), https://order.proquest.com/OA_HTML/pqdtibeCCtpItmDspRte.jsp

[13] John Bates Clark, *The Distribution of Wealth: A Theory of Wages, Interest, and Profits*, (New York: The Macmillan Company, 1899), 9.

Appendix A

The Lagrange Formulation and Sheppard Lemmas

Productions function with multiple variables.

Q = f (vi) for vi > 0

The Lagrange equation with related costs of production

L= f (vi)-(y-(c.vi)) = 0

Minimization condition,

First order condition,

$$\frac{\partial L}{\partial t} = 0$$

Second order condition,

$$\frac{\partial L^2}{\partial t} \geq 0$$

Maximization condition,

First order condition,

$$\frac{\partial L}{\partial t} = 0$$

Second order condition,

$$\frac{\partial L^2}{\partial t} \leq 0$$

Thus

$$fvi\ fvn > (fvi\ vn)^2$$

For

$$\forall\ Vi > 0 \quad (i = 1, 2, 3, \ldots n)$$

Appendix B

Permission letter

Dr. Bahman Fakhraie,
FERDAT Publishing c/o
1120 Canyon Rd # 29
Ogden, UT. , USA, 84112
E-Mail: [Not for bulk mail] bf9@utah.edu,
dr.bahf.econ@gmail.com

Dear _ (Ms/Mrs):

Date, month/ day/ year

I am completing a doctoral dissertation at __________ The Assoc. University "_______________I would like your permission to reprint in my dissertation, or research work leading to adaptation in my dissertation excerpts (beyond reference citations) from the following:
Insert full citation if any (note the same in the footnotes, or endnotes, or reference citations) and description of the original work

The excerpts to be reproduced if legally notable and beyond fair use act are:
[insert detailed explanation, or excerpts] , [or an attach sample copy of excerpts] ~

The requested permission extends to any and all "fair use" and future revisions, forms, and editions of my research works, and dissertation, including non-exclusive world rights in all languages, and to the prospective publication of my dissertation. These rights will in no way restrict republication of your copy righted materials in any other

form by you or by others authorized by you. Your signing of this letter will also confirm that you own [or your company owns] the copyright to the above-described material. I do respect your prompt objections given the legal grounds for it, otherwise, citations may be dropped, or critiques of it expanded to meet fair use act.
If these arrangements meet with your approval, please sign this letter where indicated below and return it to me in the enclosed return envelope. Thank you very much.

Sincerely, Bahman
Fakhraie

PERMISSION GRANTED FOR THE USE REQUESTED ABOVE:

Date: ____/______/______

[Name of company] :
Title:__________________ Address:
(Enclose page as needed)

Legal Notices:

F. For Time Donation, And Charity Events:1. ≤ 5% of Net 2. Time By Appointments Only. 3. Write Donations Checks to: Fakhraie Trust fund / Bahman Fakhraie

G. Any and All Risks or Harms invokes these legal clauses. The Following legal clauses are base minimum, and will not limit all rights and legal protection, with uniform constitutional rights they are implied and accorded. Contractually all rights are implied and accorded. Please, read all the legal notes before using any materials. After the customary business period not to exceed 14-days, this letter may be used as proof of contract. G1. In Cases of misuse of these materials, plagiarisms, use to put at risk of harm, or to harm, (Legal, or Etc.) the firm, CEO: Mr Bahman Fakhraie, His family members, will result in $60 million legal action per each event in United States Courts/Jurisdictions determine by author or a trust set up by Mr Bahman Fakhraie. Also, use of creative ideas intellectual properties, market front running and saturation, expansions of outlines, attempts to defraud, over charge, harm with illegal acts, misuse of private and confidential materials and properties, letters, e-mails, faxes, any and all communications, and any electronically stored materials and pictures, or false claims and defamatory media coverage against the above entities will be an agreement with all elements of this contract, and as a use license, without nullifying ensuing legal actions or collections, or as directed by the same or authorities and s. t. G1. against the above entities will be an agreement with all elements of this contract, and as a use license, without nullifying ensuing legal actions or collections, or as directed by the same or authorities. Please, notify firm, Mr. Bahman Fakhraie, of any and all infractions, transactions, or transfer to individuals or to private or government entities. G2a. All Costs due to inquiries, related or required business licenses, legal paper works and hours, all costs related to corrective or repertory publicity, bonding and insurances costs, stock related activities, all costs related to any harm (financial legal) will be charges to the sources and inquirers, and none to the firm or Bahman Fakhraie, his family, or any and all of their related assets. All attempts to harm, engagements, cashing checks or accepting cash from the same entities is an agreement with all elements of this contract. G2b. All copyrights associated with written works and further development of all works remains with the author Bahman Fakhraie or his trusts. Any and all development rights are reserved by the same entities. G3. Any and all unsolicited commercial phone calls to Mr.

Bahman Fakhraie, his family will result to a minimum of $ 500 per call charged to the source, due and payable in the same month the call is made, all other elements of this contract also apply, all contracts remain subservient to this contract, all costs of collection and legal actions also are added to the bill payable by source and not Bahman Fakhraie and these entities. G4. All Consultation and coaching involves risks due to market, business, political, etc. Costs and damages related to all such risk are paid by individuals or business entities involved and none is implied or taken by Bahman Fakhraie, his family, or any related assets, under any and all conditions. These entities' court fee are $10,000, et minimum. G5. Uncomfortable conditions, misapplications of any law to harm, harassment, odd-hour calls, etc. will be due cause for termination of services without refund, and are actionable per this contract.

®§©

Appendix C

Permission to use small quotations with notice from this work

My Name is:
January 25, 2013
Dept. /Company
Address & E-Mail, Fax, Phone
Dear Bahman Fakhraie :
I am completing a doctoral dissertation/work at

____
The Assoc. University "
. "
I would like your permission to reprint in my dissertation, or research works leading to adaptation in my dissertation excerpts (beyond reference citations) from the following, which will credit you for the copyright:
Insert full citation if any (note the same in the footnotes, or endnotes, or reference citations) and description of the original work:
The excerpts to be reproduced if legally notable and beyond fair use act are:
[insert detailed explanation, or excerpts] , [or an attach sample copy of excerpts] ~
If these arrangements meet with your approval, please sign this letter where indicated below and return it to me in the enclosed return envelope. Thank you very much.

Sincerely,

Signatory
PERMISSION GRANTED FOR THE USE REQUESTED ABOVE:
Date: ____/______/______
[Name of company]:
Title:_________________Address: _Notices: F. For

Time Donation, And Charity Events: 1. $\leq$5% of Net 2. Time By Appointments Only.

3. Write Donations Checks to: Fakhraie Trust fund / Bahman Fakhraie

G. Any and All Risks or Harms invokes these legal clauses. The Following legal clauses are base minimum, and will not limit all rights and legal protection, with uniform constitutional rights they are implied and accorded. Contractually all rights are implied and accorded. Please, read all the legal notes before using any materials.

G1. In Cases of misuse of these materials, plagiarisms, use to put at risk of harm, or to harm, (Legal, or Etc.) the firm, CEO: Mr. Bahman Fakhraie, His family members, will result in $60 million legal action per each event in United States Courts/ any Jurisdictions determined or set by author or a trust set up by Mr. Bahman Fakhraie. Also, use of creative ideas and intellectual properties for any commerce direct or indirect or by proxy, expansions of outlines, attempts to defraud, over charge, harm with illegal acts, misuse of private and confidential materials, information, and properties, letters, checks, e-mails, faxes, any and all communications, and any electronically stored materials and pictures, or false claims against the above entities will be an agreement with and subject to all elements of this contract, and as a use license, without nullifying further and ensuing legal actions or collections, or as directed by the same or authorities. All other contracts are one time contracts and s. t. this contract. Please, notify firm, Mr. Bahman Fakhraie, of any and all infractions, transactions, or transfer to individuals or to private or government entities in accord with current laws.

G2a. All Costs due to inquiries, related or required business licenses, legal paper works and hours, all costs related to corrective or reparation publicity, bonding and insurances costs, stock related activities, all costs related to any harm (financial legal) will be charges to the sources and inquirers, and none to the firm or Bahman Fakhraie, his family, or any and all of their related assets. All attempts to harm, engagements, cashing checks or accepting cash from the same entities is an agreement with all elements of this contract.

G2b. All copy rights associated with written works and further development of all works remains with the author Bahman Fakhraie or his trusts. Any and all development rights are reserved by the same entities.

G3. Any and all unsolicited commercial phone calls to Mr. Bahman Fakhraie, his family will result to a minimum of $ 500 per call charged to the source, due and payable in the same month the call is made, all other elements of this contract also apply, all contracts remain subservient to this contract, all costs of collection and legal actions also are added to the bill payable by source and not Bahman Fakhraie and these entities.

G4. All Consultation and coaching involves risks due to market, business, political, etc. costs and damages related to all such risk are paid by individuals or business entities involved and none is implied or taken by Bahman Fakhraie, his family, or any related assets, under any and all conditions. These entities' court fees are $10,000, et minimum.

G5. Uncomfortable conditions, misapplications of any law to harm, harassment, odd-hour calls, etc. will be due cause for termination of services without refund, and are actionable.

®§©

Appendix D

Legal Notes

All Right Reserved & Other Legal Notes

E. Speech, Lecture Tours, Research Papers & Follow Up:

1. Per Each Event. . . . . $ 100,000
2. With Foreign Travel. . . . . $ 3,000,000
3. Book/Cash Advance $600,000, Net Royalties ~40%
4. Scripts: /Starting from. . . . . $ 100,000
5. a, Movie Script (120+Pages). .. . . $ 3,000,000
5. b, Or Cash Advance Plus 2% of All Gross paid annually
6. Consultations Fee/Initial charge non-refunded $ 1000, & 10 %
7. Business limited ventures, partnerships, etc. . $ 30%
8. Any and All Risks or Harms invokes Sec. G

F. For Time Donation, And Charity Events: a. 5% of Net, Time By Appointments Only.

G. Any and All Risks or Harms invokes these legal clauses. The Following legal clauses are base minimum, and will not limit all rights and legal protection, with uniform constitutional rights they are implied and accorded. Contractually all rights are implied and accorded. Please, read all the legal notes before using any materials. After the customary business period not to exceed 14-days, this letter may be used as proof of contract. G1. In Cases of misuse of these materials, plagiarisms, use to put at risk of harm, or to harm, (Legal, or Etc.) the firm, CEO: Mr. Bahman Fakhraie, His family members, will result in $60 million legal action per each event in United States Courts/Jurisdictions determine by author or a trust set up by Mr. Bahman Fakhraie. Also, use of creative ideas intellectual properties, market front running and saturation, expansions of outlines, attempts to defraud, over charge, harm with illegal acts, misuse of private and confidential materials and properties, letters, e-mails, faxes, any and all communications, and any electronically stored materials and pictures, or false claims and defamatory media coverage against the above entities will be an agreement with all elements of this contract, and as a use license, without nullifying ensuing legal actions or collections, or as directed by the same or authorities and s. t. G1. against the above entities will be an agreement with all elements of this contract, and as a use license, without nullifying ensuing legal actions or collections, or as directed by the same or authorities. Please, notify firm, Mr. Bahman Fakhraie, of any and all infractions, transactions, or transfer to individuals or to private or government entities. G2a. All Costs due to inquiries, related or required business licenses, legal paper works and hours, all costs related to corrective or repertory publicity, bonding and insurances costs, stock related activities, all costs related to any harm (financial legal) will be charges to the sources and inquirers, and none to the firm or Bahman Fakhraie, his family, or any and all of their related assets. All attempts to harm, engagements, cashing checks or accepting cash from the same entities is an agreement with all elements of this contract. G2b. All copy rights associated with written works and further development of all works remains with the author Bahman Fakhraie or his trusts. Any and all development rights are reserved by the same entities. G3. Any and all unsolicited commercial phone calls to Mr. Bahman Fakhraie, his family will result to a minimum of $ 500 per call charged to the source, due and payable in the same month the call is made, all other elements of this contract also apply, all contracts remain subservient to this contract, all costs of collection and legal actions also are added to the bill payable by source and not Bahman Fakhraie and these entities. G4. All Consultation and coaching involves risks due to market, business, political, etc. costs and damages related to all such risk are paid by individuals or business entities involved and none is implied or taken by Bahman Fakhraie, his family, or any related assets, under any and all conditions. These entities' court fee are $10,000, set minimum. G5. Uncomfortable conditions, misapplications of any law to harm, harassment, odd-hour calls, etc. will be due cause for termination of services without refund, and are actionable per this contract.

®§©

Appendix E

FERDAT's, Budgetary, Managerial Directive, and

Legal Clauses

(Continues)

FERDT

FERDAT

Fakhraie Education Research

Development And Trust

Organization, Fakhraie Bahman

Grant proposal by

Budgetary, Managerial

Directive,

Legal letter and charges for

unauthorized information use.

Section 1, Mission Statement

Section 2, Budgetary Clause

Section 3, Managerial Clause

Section 4, Legal Clause

Section 5, Organization Chart

Section 6, Data Management

Legal letter is in cases of e-fraud, misuse of firms' information, or harm under sec. G. All linked and relaying entities, institutions, governmental agencies are accountable no exception.

Dear Sirs, persons, INC., (illegal use of firms' info), your current bill is **$10,000, ≤Ceiling $60 mils.** On behalf of Dr. Bahman Fakhraie, FERDAT, and the firm, family trusts.
These are the current charges related to illegal e-fraud and all harmful misuse of firms information, after the first time we asked you to terminate all contract and remove our name, firms' name etc. on this date.

1-Illegal use, the unapproved initial use of firm's name, contact name, duns #, any and all information supplied to USA government for the soul purpose of firm doing business with USA government, grant.gov, and NSF, Universities, other governmental and tribal entities, and all grantors. Minimum charges are $10,000.00, up to the ceiling of $ 60 million.

2-Use of firm contacts, names, address phone #, TIN/#s, and any information related to that.

Minimum charges are $10,000.00, up to the ceiling of $60 mils.

3- Continuation after repeated formal request to terminate illegal actions, sending junk e-mail, junk mail, forcing this firm to send back, by mail and certified mail. Legal costs related to that.

Minimum charges are $10,000.00 per each event, up to the ceiling of $60 mils.

4- Interference with firm soul business, time sensitive writing of government and private grants, at grant.gov, and NSF, universities, private foundations, NGOs and all grantors, with 4.5 million dollars floor. The Minimum charges are 4.5 million dollars, up to the ceiling of $60 mils.

4- Absolut or required non-disclosures by the firm or Dr. Fakhraie will require pre-paid plan with minimum flooring pay. Flex-legalism targeted at the firm, or Dr. B. Fakhraie will be due cause for nonpaid termination by the same, and harm-terms of Sec G of private contracts.

6- Punitive damages are up to 60 million dollars, if you do not stop, after the first notification.

Please make an effort to pay your bill. There will be additional charges added and sent to you for each time you try to contact the same entities, after the same dated termination notices.

Dr. BF, this is part of the legal notices under sec G, or formal termination notice dates.

Section 1, Mission Statement

To formulate optimum functionality in management teams, in order to make profitable and beneficial contributions, and create opportunity for merited advancements, **to advance research** in my fields of study. Utilizing rare combination of theory and empiricism, cultivated in multi-cultural inclusive settings in academic and private enterprises, I enhance the management in productivity and completion of productive projects, or suggest corrective recursive evaluation and total quality control improvements.

Experiences, among fields of International Trade, Managerial, and Production theories in Economics, Finance, Personal Finance management, and Businesses, which modern business and academic institutions find very expensive to employ and too costly not to employ. My extensive background help me advance research in my fields of study.

Section 2, Budgetary Clause

* All initial dedicated deposits (inflows) will be transferred to a FREDT, or FREDAT business account.

* No allotments or contracts activity will take place, until full transfer of funds has taken place per contracts. The cash-accounting method is used for tax purposes.

* Alteration to submit to requirements and regulations will fully transfer all risks, fees, and penalties, and legal

responsibilities, to the source of the requirements.

* There will be a minimum product list, or writing, or proposal-output for further research, which will be presented and agreed to at the initial phases.

* This will be the only output legally required at the end of contract, or at the end of grant periods.

* There is a managerial flow chart enclosed to enhance comprehensions of cash flow, read after the legal notes section.

Section 3, Managerial Clause

* Dr Bahman Fakhraie will act as agent, manger, and soul administrator, Executives director, Principle Investigator PI for FERDT, FERDAT, Fakhraie Bahman Organization, with full rights to take legal action and make final settlement on its accounts.

* Dr Bahman Fakhraie will act as agent, manger, and soul administrator for Fakhraie Bahman Organization, with full right to take legal action on its accounts.

* A general electronic bookkeeping is followed, on periodical bases, as grants require it. Current standard is quarterly,

post full disbursements of grant funding. (FRR is required quarterly)

* Details, information, managerial technologies are legally protected, and no such disclosure will be made of the Organization, administrator, assignees, or representatives of FERDT, FERDAT, or Fakhraie Bahman Organization. All copyright materials are marketable, or further developed by Mr. Fakhraie. All existing rights are reserved.

* All informal and formal requests can be made by mail, or email.

* There is forfeiture of all advances, in cases of mortality, health, or attempt at disbarment, legal action, harm, against soul administrator, Fakhraie Bahman Organization, with full right to take legal action on its accounts.

* Any and all such request will have to forward additional funding for legal representations and undue imposition of costs or harm, please read the legal note and sec. G. It will always apply.

* Alteration to submit to requirements and regulations will fully transfer all risks, fees, and penalties, and legal responsibilities, to the source of the requirements.

* The reviewers will have access to a portion of the progress.

* Full transparencies are practiced for authorized agents only, mostly through the Internet, after proper signatures are obtained.

* All future development, educational development will have to be contracted, or signed out temporarily.

* All copyrights and proprietary rights are reserved, granted, accorded to Dr Bahman Fakhraie, and his living trust.

* The final product in initial agreement will be shared with the grantors, after all the financial settlements have been met.

* PI, FERDAT; Fakhraie, Bahman

  Dr. Bahman Fakhraie, PhD, UOU, UT, USA

* Position Classification, Executive level I,

* Salary exceeds Fed Cap for private contracts.

* NSF ID, xxxxx6796,

* Organizational ID Code, P xxxxx8425

* Private for Profit Business:

* DUNS Number D&B # xxxxx89684,

* CAGE/NCAGE: 692S3, Congressional Districts, UT_001

* Sec G of private contract always applies

* For institutional DUNS, etc. Please, check cover letter, or contact PI. Thanks

* UOU PI Information

□ Federal Interagency Committee on Education (FICE) Code for the U: **003675**

□ EIN. TAX ID/TIN: **87-6000525**

□ DUNS Num: **D & B #009095365**
□ Cage Code: **3T 624**
□ NSF Institutional Code: **36756000**
□ NIH Institutional Code: **514002**
□ Congressional District: **UT-002**
□ Type of Organization: **State Institution of Higher Education**
□ AAALAC Accreditation: **8 March 2000 - (Animal Resource Center Facilities and Programs Accreditation)**
□ USDA Registration Number (Animal Subject): **87-R-0001**
□ PHS Animal Welfare Assurance ID Number: **A3031-01**
□ Human Subjects Federal Wide Assurance: **FWA00003745 (expires 11.06.2011)**
□ Effective Date of Cost Accounting Statement: **Disclosure Statement submitted 12.31.97 (not yet audited or approved by**
* **DHHS)**

Section 4, Legal Clause, All Right Reserved & Other Legal Notes

E. Speech, Lecture Tours, and Research Papers & Follow Up:

All publications or Grant-products are commonly published on completion, USA Library of Congress, Trade Journals, Or Author's websites, etc.

Contact for individualized contracts

F. For Time Donation, And Charity Events: 1. 5% of Net contracts paid 2. Time By Appointments Only.3. Write Donations Checks to: Fakhraie Trust fund / Bahman Fakhraie

G. Any and All Risks or Harms invokes these legal clauses. The Following legal clauses are base minimum, and will not limit all rights and legal protection, with uniform constitutional rights they are implied and accorded. Contractually all rights are implied and accorded. Please, read all the legal notes before using any materials.

G1. In Cases of misuse of these materials, plagiarisms, use to put at risk of harm, or to harm, (Legal, or Etc.) the firm, CEO, FERDT, president: Mr. Bahman Fakhraie, His family members, it will result in $60 million legal action per each event in United States Courts/ any Jurisdictions determined or set by author or a trust set up by Mr. Bahman Fakhraie. Also, use of creative ideas and intellectual properties for any commerce direct or indirect or by proxy, expansions of outlines, attempts to defraud, over charge, harm with illegal acts, misuse of private and confidential materials, information, and properties, letters, checks, e-mails, faxes, any and all communications, and any electronically stored materials and pictures, or false claims against the above entities will be an agreement with and subject to all elements of this contract, and as a user license, without nullifying further and ensuing legal actions or collections, or as directed by the same or authorities. All other contracts are one time contracts and s. t. this contract. Please, notify firm, Mr. Bahman Fakhraie, of all infractions, transactions, or transfer to individuals or to private or government entities in accord with current laws.

G2a. All Costs due to inquiries, related or required business licenses, legal paper works, and hours, all costs related to corrective or reparation publicity, bonding and insurances costs, stock related activities, all costs related to any harm (financial & legal) will be charges to the sources and inquirers, and none to the firm or Bahman Fakhraie, his family, or any and all of their related assets. All attempts to harm, engagements, cashing checks or accepting cash from the same entities is an agreement with all elements of this contract.

G2b. All copy rights associated with written works and further development of all works remains with the author Bahman Fakhraie or his trusts. All development rights are reserved by the same entities.

G3. Any and all unsolicited commercial phone calls, to Mr. Bahman Fakhraie and , his family will result to a minimum of $ 500 per call charged to the source, due and payable in the same month the call is made, all other elements of this contract also apply, all contracts remain subservient to this contract, all costs of collection and legal actions also are added to the bill payable by source and not Bahman Fakhraie and these entities.

G4.All Consultation and coaching involves risks due to market, business, political, etc. costs and damages related to all such risk are paid by individuals or business entities involved and none is implied or taken by Bahman Fakhraie, his family, or any related assets, under any and all conditions. These entities' court fees are $10,000; et minimum.

G5.Uncomfortable conditions, misapplications of any law to harm, harassment, odd-hour calls, etc will be due cause for termination of services without refund, and are actionable per this contract.

§§§§

All Right Reserved & Other Legal Notes

All publications or Grant-products are published on completion, USA Library of Congress, Trade Journals, Or Author's websites, etc.

E. Speech, Lecture Tours, Research Papers & Follow Up:

1. Per Each Event-$ 350,000 +.
2. with Foreign Travel-$ 3,000,000
3. Book/Cash Advance $6,000,000; Net Royalties ~40%
4. Scripts: /Starting from....................$ 300,000
5. Movie Script (120+Pages)................$ 3,000,000
6. Or Cash Advance Plus 2% of All Gross paid annually
7. Consultations Fee/Initial charge non-refunded $ 10,000, & ...10 %
8. Business limited ventures, partnerships, etc. .... □ 30%
9. Salary executive level I

F. For Time Donation, And Charity Events: 1. 5% of Net contracts paid 2. Time By Appointments Only.3. Write Donations Checks to Fakhraie Trust fund / Bahman Fakhraie. G. Any and All Risks or Harms invokes these legal clauses. The Following legal clauses are base minimum, and will not limit all rights and legal protection, with uniform constitutional rights they are implied and accorded. Contractually all rights are implied and accorded. Please, read all the legal notes before using any materials. G1. In Cases of misuse of these materials, plagiarisms, use to put at risk of harm, or to harm, (Legal, or Etc.) the firm, CEO: Mr. Bahman Fakhraie, His family members, will result in $60 million legal action per each event in United States Courts/Jurisdictions determine by author or a trust set up by Mr. Bahman Fakhraie. Also, use of creative ideas intellectual properties, expansions of outlines, attempts to defraud, over charge, harm with illegal acts, misuse of private and confidential materials and properties, letters, e-mails, faxes, any and all communications, and any electronically stored materials and pictures, or false claims against the above entities will be an agreement with all elements of this contract, and as a use license, without nullifying ensuing legal actions or collections, or as directed by the same or authorities. Please, notify firm, Mr. Bahman Fakhraie, of any and all infractions, transactions, or transfer to individuals or to private or government entities. G2a. All Costs due to inquiries, related or required business licenses, legal paper works and hours, all costs related to corrective or reparation publicity, bonding and insurances costs, stock related activities, all costs related to any harm (financial & legal) will be charges to the sources and inquirers, and none to the firm or Bahman Fakhraie, his family, or any and all of their related assets. All attempts to harm, engagements, cashing checks or accepting cash from the same entities is an agreement with all elements of this contract. G2b. All copy rights associated with written works and further development of all works remains with the author Bahman Fakhraie or his trusts. Any and all development rights are reserved by the same entities. G3. Any and all unsolicited commercial phone calls to Mr. Bahman Fakhraie, his family will result to a minimum of $ 500 per call charged to the source, due and payable in the same month the call is made, all other elements of this contract also apply, all contracts remain subservient to this contract, all costs of collection and legal actions also are added to the bill payable by source and not Bahman Fakhraie and these entities. G4.All Consultation and coaching involves risks due to market, business, political, etc. costs and damages related to all such risk are paid by individuals or business entities involved and none is implied or taken by Bahman Fakhraie, his family, or any related assets, under any and all conditions. These entities' court fees are $10,000; et minimum. G5.Uncomfortable conditions, misapplications of any law to harm, harassment, odd-hour calls, etc will be due cause for termination of services without refund, and are actionable per this contract.

§§§§

Letter of Agreement with FRDET and Fakhraie Bahman

I/We (Ms, Mrs, Mr):

Business Name:

Social Security numbers:
........../......./................ ..../......./................

Tax ID Numbers:
....

Driver License Numbers:
....

Passport (Birth Certificate) Numbers:
....

Have read all the information supplied by Mr Bahman Fakhraie, and /or FRDET (Trust, LLP). Agree to supply all correct financial and related information and select the following services by marking (X), or Letter a b c, Or Number 1 2 3, or write and specify. Agree to the power of attorney required to confirm or acquire financial and related information. Plus a check for $3000, for preliminary registrations, legal and financial inquiries, and licensing fees.

1: □□□□□□□□2: □□□□□□□ 3: □□□□□□□□□
4:□□□□□□□□ 5: □□□□□□□□6: □□□□□□□7: □ 8: □

Specify which kinds of the following accounts you will require:

Individual/Gov. □ □ Joints □ □
Joint with survival rights □ Trusts □□

Details:

Business types:

Ltd Partnership (LLP, LLC) □ □ Soul Owner □ □ Inc/Gov □ Firm □ □

Details:

I/We agree to pay the fees and costs as they accrue, after 30 days a charge of %10 per annum is added to past due amounts until they are settled or paid in full. That at least 75% charges and expenses are paid no later than six month after initial reports or outlines are examined. That all travel lodgings and phone charges, legal research, and research hours, I/We request are fully paid. I/We have read and understand the nature of business, business cycles, market price fluctuation risks, currency fluctuation risks, social and political risks, natural and climatic risks, and all other risks herewith not itemized; therefore, I/we accept all financial losses, responsibilities, all punitive or compensatory damages that occur for all activities that are undertaken based on or claimed related to the report or reports, advise and etc., generated by Money Wise Firm, Bahman Fakhraie or all the entities named, agents, and associates. I/We understand in cases of any false, misleading, or withholding information the Money Wise Firm and all entities named above will not be held accountable, responsible, financially or otherwise, and will be refunded for any damages fully. I/We release all others associated with Money Wise Firm, and Bahman Fakhraie from financial losses, responsibilities, all compensatory and punitive charges concerning activities I/We undertake.

Sign (full name, titles, and address)

Business (Name, Address; Agents' title):

Section 5, Organization Chart

⇔Requests for grants, grant and contract proposals and Minimums contracted output Grant Funds,

⇓ Organization DUNS, University DUNS ⇓

Administrator ⇒FRDAT

⇓

FERDAT-C

Publishing and Production

President, Administrator, Executive level 1

⇓

Bahman Fakhraie, PhD, © 2011, UOU, UT, USA ®, ™

⇓

Tasks and controls, TQC, and Redo, Recycles

⇔Tax and expense disbursements

⇓

Completed project Vs. Minimums contracted output

⇔ Informal notification of source of funds, with future project proposal if any,

⇒Formal and final notification from FRDET, FERDAT

⇔ Final confirmation of conclusion from Administrators

⇒ Final confirmation of conclusion from Organization Fakhraie

⇔ Keeping communication and net work open to future project.

Section 6, DATA MANAGEMENT:

Relevant data will be managed, and stored.

Moreover, the data and the progression of data used will be stored post completion.

As a common practice, Dr Bahman Fakhraie will, also preserve a historical over view of data for legal purposes, for future use. A portion of that will be shared if requested in written form, post settlement of all expenses.

The ethical requirements will be followed in accordance with the applied law established.

The final product will be shared with the grantors, after all the financial settlements have been met. The reviewers will have access to a portion of the progress.

All publications or Grant-products are published on completion, USA Library of Congress, Trade Journals, FERDAT Publishing, Or Author's websites, etc.

Labor laws and benefit distribution will be according to the institutional Fed Cap limits, private contracts; vendors are responsible for their own legal obligations. (Publication Ink, FedExx, kinkcos, vendors etc.)

CPA and Legal establishment, outside to this entity will be contracted to handle more complex issues when they arise, all cost are due, prior to any such required actions are requested.

Full transparencies are practiced for authorized agents only, mostly through the internet, after proper signatures are obtained. All copyrights and proprietary rights are granted, accorded and reserved to Dr Bahman Fakhraie,

All future development, educational development will have to be contracted, or signed out temporarily, they will revert to Dr. Bahman Fakhraie, in case of any and all legal issues.

These and other clauses will be amended and upgraded as required over time, they all apply.

Absolut or required non-disclosures by the firm or Dr. Fakhraie will require pre-paid plan with minimum flooring pay. Flex-legalism targeted at the firm, or Dr. B. Fakhraie will be due cause for nonpaid termination by the same.

G. Any and All Risks or Harms invokes these legal clauses. The Following legal clauses are base minimum, and will not limit all rights and legal protection, with uniform constitutional rights they are implied and accorded. Contractually all rights are implied and accorded. Please, read all the legal notes before using any materials.

Section 7, Vita

Bahman Fakhraie, PH.D. University Of Utah

Economic Dept., Salt Lake City, Utah USA, 84112

Permanent Address: c/o 1120 Canyon Rd #29; Ogden Utah 84404-7663

E-Mail: bf9@utah.edu , bahf.econ@gmail.com

Honors and Awards: Omicron Delta Epsilon Honor Society
Student leadership positions: President of International Student Association
Bachelor of Science: Utah State University
Master of Science: Utah State University
PhD, University of Utah University of Utah
Mission Statement:

To formulate optimum functionality in management teams, in order to make profitable and beneficial contributions, and create opportunity for merited advancements.

Utilizing rare combination of theory and empiricism, cultivated in multi-cultural inclusive settings in academic and private enterprise, I enhance the management in productivity and completion of productive projects, or suggest corrective recursive evaluation and total quality control improvements.

Experiences, among fields of International Trade, Managerial, and Production theories in Economics, Finance, Personal Finance and Business, which modern business and academic institutions find very expensive to employ and too costly not to employ. The extensive background helps advance research in my fields of study.

Goals:

I have initiated, passed, and funded many constructive projects --goals by committees--, where it has been value enhancing and mutually beneficial individually, and by team assists.
Private Senior Economist: Research Positions with Contracts, Teaching, Research, Books, with contract. Short Term Private Contracts are for economic and financial educational consultations.
Academic Preparatory Continuum:
PhD, University of Utah

Dissertation:
TECHNOLOGICAL INJECTION, DYNAMIC NEW CAPITAL MEASUREMENTS,
AND PRODUCTION THEORY IN ECONOMICS

Dr. Bahman Fakhraie's Book-link is at,
https://order.proquest.com/OA_HTML/pqdtibeCCtpItmDspRte.jsp

Thesis statement:

The dynamic influences of technology and elemental factors of production --defined and measured in this dissertation-- are greater than commonly have been calculated or expected. The impacts of different measurements of capital stocks (traditional and new adjusted capital) on embodied and disembodied technological variables, on productivity, and economic growth of national social products are tested. The econometric effects of two new capital stock measures introduced in the writing of Friedrich August Von Hayek, John Maynard Keynes, and further developed by Evsey D. Domar, and ignored by most modern economists are examined. Therefore, we focus on the demand and supply side of technological embodied in capital, in human skill and produced goods and services, and the economy.

Post-Doctoral Goals:

1. Updating the econometrics of the dissertation to most recent available data and dates. (per available grants)

2. Include, countries, with acceptable data in the study, set up formulaic development in excel etc for use.(per grants)

3. Focus on the theoretical advancement in production processes for systemic innovational additive methodologies, in Movie production, Agriculture, and other creative industries, using existing or newly hired faculties, in anchored and linked institutions. This is a great serious work in shadows of Adam Smith, Schumpeter, Hayak, and Keynes.

4. Stream line methodologies, and project for PhD Students, master students, and introductory fields' level, an extension of the dissertation and current copyrighted writings.

5. Of course, this will be under Sec G of private contract and without infringing on rights of marketing, publishing, and distribution of the same. Certain contracts will be more restrictive, including specific names.

Production theory in Agriculture

Agro-production, Sheep production in Iran (an onsite research project 1975)

Monetary Macroeconomic Specialization (Milton Freedman,)

International Monetary macroeconomic Specializations (Robert Mundell)

Fiscal Analysis of oscillatory modifications

Applied Agricultural production in developing economies

Inappropriate Technology Transfers by Corporations and dualistic induced instabilities in pre-democratic economies.

SELECTED BIBLIOGRAPHY

Bailey, Martin J., *National Income and the Price Level: A Study in Macroeconomic Theory,* New York: McGraw-Hill, 1971.

Baumol, William J., *Economic Theory and Operational Analysis,* 4th ed., New Jersey: Prentice-Hall, 1977.

Blaug, Mark., *Economic Theory in Retrospect,* 3rd Ed., London: The Cambridge University Press, 1978.

Böhn_Bawerk, Eugen Von., *Capital and Interest: Positive Theory of Capital,* vol. II, Trans. G. D. Hunt & H. F. Sennholz, Chicago: Libertarian Press, 1959.

Boulding, Kenneth E., *Economics As A science*, New York: McGraw-Hill Book Company, 1970.

Byers, Lloyd L., *Concept of Strategic Management: Planning and Implementation*, New York: Harper & Row Publishers.

Caves, Richard E. and Jones, R. W., *World Trade and Payments: An Introduction*, 2nd ed., Boston: Little, Brown and Company, 1977.

Chiang, Alpha C., *Fundamental Methods of Mathematical Economics*, 2nd ed., New York: McGraw-Hill Book Company, 1974.

Coombs, Philip H., *The World Educational Crisis: A System Analysis*, London: Oxford University Press, 1968.

Domar, Evsey D., *Essays in the Theory of Economic Growth*, New York: Oxford University Press, 1957, 154-167, 168, 181.

Druker, Peter F., *Innovation and Entrepreneurship*, New York: Harper & Row Publishers, 1985.

Eisner, R. "Depreciation Allowances, Replacement Requirement, and Growth," *The American Economic Review*, XLII, December 1952.

Fakhraie, Bahman, "The Demand and Supply Sides of Appropriate Technological Advancement." (Research paper at University of Utah Economics Dept. 2003)

—. *Technological injection, dynamic new capital measurements, and Production Theory in Economics*, (Michigan: ProQuest LLC, 2010) , https://order.proquest.com/OA_HTML/pqdtibeCCtpItmDspRte.jsp, http://www.amazon.com/Technological-injection-measurements-production-economics/dp/1244628506, http://www.barnesandnoble.com/s/Bahman-Fakhraie?keyword=Bahman+Fakhraie&store=book

—. "Economic Theories and Practices in Technological Changes, capital measures, and Production." (Research paper at University of Utah Economics Dept. 1988)

—. "Hallowing headless nations?: the need to invest on public education under the 1980s international economic conditions," (Research paper at University of Utah Economics Dept. 1988)

—. "Transfer of Technologies and Socioeconomic Theories of Dualism," (Research paper at University of Utah Economics Dept. 1983)

Friedman, Milton and Schwartz, Anna Jacobson, *The Great Contraction 1929-1933*, vol.2, 2nd ed., New Jersey: Princeton University Press, 1973

Gander, James Patrick., *Technological Change and Raw Materials*, Salt Lake City: Bureau of Economic and Business Research, University of Utah, 1977.

Gardner, Ackley., *Macroeconomics: Theory and Policy*, New York: Macmillan Publishing Co., 1978.

Girton, Lance and Roper Don, "Theory and Implication of Currency Substitution," *Journal of Money, Credit, and Banking,* 13, no. 1 (February 1981): 12-30.

Hayek, Friedrich August Von. , "Kapitalaufzehrung." Weltwirtschaftliches Archive 36, 1932, II, 86-108.

Heilbroner, Robert L., *The Worldly Philosophers*, New York: Time Inc., Special Ed., 1962.

Hicks, Sir John, *The Crisis in Keynesian Economics*, New York: Basic Books, Inc. 1974.

Hirshleifer, Jack, *Investment, Interest, and Capital*, New Jersey: Prentice-Hall, 1970.

—. *Time, Uncertainty, and Information*, New York: Basil Blackwell, 1989.

—. *Price Theory and Applications*, New Jersey: Prentice-Hall, 1976.

Henderson, J. M. and Quandt, R. E., *Microeconomic Theory; A Mathematical Approach*, 2nd ed., New York: McGraw-Hill, 1972. 191-199, 280

Hunt, E. K. and Howard J. Sherman, Economics*: An Introduction to Traditional and Radical Views*, 2nd Ed., San Francisco: Harper and Row Publishers, 1975.

Intriligator, Michael D., *Econometric Models, Techniques, and Applications*, New Jersey: Prentice-Hall, 1978.

Johnson, J., *Econometric Methods*. New York: McGraw-Hill, 1972.

Kant, Immanuel, *Critique of Judgment*, Trans. J. H. Bernard, New York: Hafner, 1951.

Kennedy Charles and Thirlwall, A.P., "Surveys in Applied Economics: Technological Progress," *The Economic Journal*, March, 1972, 12.

Keynes, John Maynard, *Essays in Biography*, London: The Cambridge University Printing House for Royal Economic Society, 1972.

—. *The General Theory of Employment, Interest and Money,* 1st ed. 1936, London: The Cambridge University Printing House for Royal Economic Society, Reprint 1973.

Kindleberger, Charles P., *The World in Depression 1929-1939*, Los Angeles: University of California Press, 1973.

Kirzner, I.M., *Discovery and the Capitalist Process*, Chicago: University of Chicago Press, 1985.

Klein, P. A. and Moore, G. H., *Monitoring Growth Cycles in Market-Oriented Countries*, (Mass.: published for N. B. E. R., by Ballinger publishing Co., 1985).

Knight, Farnk H., *Risk, Uncertainty and Profit*, Chicago: University of Chicago Press, 1985.

Landes, David S., *The wealth and poverty of nations: Why Some are So Rich and Some are So Poor*, (New York: W.W. Norton & Company, 1998).

Lindert, Peter H. and Kindleberger Charles P., *International Economics,* 7th Ed., Illinois: Richard Irwin, 1982.

Mansfield, Edwin, *Technological Change*, New York: W. W. Norton & Co., 1971.

Mark, Blaug, *Economic Theory in Retrospect*, 3rd Ed. London: The Cambridge University Press, 1978.

Marx, K. (In a letter he wrote to Engel, dated 20 August, 1862, London), (handout by Professor Randa, 2004)

McKinnon, Ronald I., *Money and Capital in Economic Development*, Washington D. C.: The Brookings Institution, 1973.

Mensch, Gerhard, Das *technilogische Patt.*, Frankfurt: Umschau Verlag, 1975.

—, *Stalemate in Technology: innovation overcome the Depression*, (Massachusetts: Ballinger Publishing Company, 1979).

Miles, T.R., "Gestalt Theory," in The Encyclopedia of Philosophy, New York: Macmillan Publishing Co., vols. 3 and 4, 1967.

Mishan, Edward Joshua, *Cost-Benefit Analysis,* 4th Ed. London: Unwin Hyman, 1988.

Moran, Michael. "New England Transcendentalism," in The Encyclopedia of Philosophy, (New York: Macmillan Publishing Co., Vols. 3 and 4, 1967).

Mundell, Robert A. , "Growth, Stability, and Inflationary Finance," Journal *of Political Economy*, 73, 1963.

Pindyck, R.S., and Rubinfeld, D.L., *Econometric Models and Econometric*, 2nd ed., New York: McGraw-Hills, 1981.

Ott, J. Steven, *The Organizational Culture Perspectives*, (Pacific Grove, California: Brooks/Cole Publishing Company, 1989).

Quirk, James and Saposnik, Rubin, *Introduction to General Equilibrium Theory and Welfare Economics*, New York: McGraw-Hill, 1968.

Rima, Ingrid, *Development of Economic Analysis*, 7th ed., New York: Routledge, 2009.

Rodinson, M., *Islam and Capitalism*, Trans. B. Pearce, Austin: University of Texas, 1981.

Rosenberg, Nathan, Technology *and American Economic Growth*, New York: M. E. Sharp, 1972.

Ruttan, V. W. , "Usher and Schumpeter on Invention, and Technological Change," Quarterly *Journal of Economics*, 1960, 602.

Ruttan, Vernon W. , "Usher and Schumpeter on Invention, Innovation, and Technological change," Quarterly *Journal of Economics*, 1960, 73.

Samuelson, Anthony Paul. Economics, 11th Ed., New York: McGraw-Hill, 1980.

Savich, R.S., and Thomson, L. A., *Resource Allocation within the Product Life Cycles*, Business Topic, MSU: MSU, fall 1978.

Schmooker, Jacob, *Invention and Economic Growth*, Massachusetts: Harvard University Press, 1966.

Schultz, Theodore W. , *Investing in People: The Economics of Population Quality*, Berkley: University of California Press, 1982.

Schumpeter, Joseph A., *Business Cycles*, vol. 1. New York: McGraw Hill Book Company, 1939.

—. *Business Cycles: A Theoretical, Historical, and Statistical Analysis of the Capitalists Process,* vol. I, New York: McGraw Hill Book Company, 1938.

—. *The Theory of Economic Development: An Inquiry into Profits, Capital, Credit, Interest, and Business Cycle*, Trans., Redvers Opie, London: Oxford University Press, Reprint 1980.

Smith, Adam., *An Inquiry into the Nature and Cause of Wealth of Nations*, Edited by E. Cannon, Chicago: University of Chicago Press, 1976.

—. *An Inquiry into the Nature and Causes of Wealth of Nations*, vol. 2, 2nd ed., Oxford: the Clarendon Press, 1988.

—. *The Theory of Moral Sentiments*, London, 1st ed., 1757.

Smith, E.J. Chambers, R.H. Scott and R.S., *National Income Analysis and Forecasting*, Glenview: Scott, Foresman and Company, 1975.

Spiegle, Henry William., *The Growth of Economic thought*, North Carolina: Duke University Press, 1983.

Stigler, George J., *The Theory of Price*, 3rd ed., New York: The Macmillan Company, 1966.

Takaki, Ronald., *A Different Mirror: A History of Multicultural America*, London: Little Brown and Company, 1993.

Taylor, John R., *An Introduction to Error Analysis*, Mill Valley: University Science Books, 1982.

Thirtle, Colin G. and Ruttan V. W., *The Role of Demand and Supply in the Generation of Diffusion of Technological Change*, Switzerland, 1987.

U. S. President, *Economic Report of the President*, (Washington, D.C.: Government printing office, 1990)

Usher, Abbot Payson, *A History of Mechanical Inventions*, London: Oxford University Press, 1954.

Usher, Abbot Payson, *A History of Mechanical Inventions,* Revised ed., London: Oxford University Press, 1954.

Viner, Jacob, *Studies in the Theories of International Trade*, New York: Harper and Brothers publishers, 1937.

Wainwright, A. C. Chiang and K., *Fundamental Methods of Mathematical Economics*, 4th ed., Boston: McGraw-Hill Irwin, 2005.

Webster, Merriam, *Merriam-Webster's Collegiate Dictionary*, 9th ed., Springfield: M.W. Inc., 1985.

Young, Hugh D., *Statistical Treatment of Experimental Data*, New York: McGraw-Hill, 1962.

Dr. Bahman Fakhraie, PhD, Economics, University of Utah, Salt Lake City Utah, BS, and MS from Utah State University, at Logan Utah. Dr. Bahman Fakhraie dissertation adds to the influences and importance of the Unorthodox-Holistic Economic analyses, or the Gestalt of Unorthodox economic doctrine, in the millennial age of technological paradigm shifts. He applies analytical and research skills with a holistic view of events, history, mathematics, and econometrics to economic analysis, with scientific background and multimedia digitized presentations for marketing. He is A Published Economist, Author, Researcher, Investor, and Private Contractor. His expertise are in international trade and finance, economic production, growth (theory and application), development theory, econometrics, (math, micro, and macro), Agriculture economics, and agronomy. He grew up working in family businesses, banking, small farm, auto agency, and shop. Dr. Bahman Fakhraie was invited by Senator Frank M. Browning of Ogden Utah to attend Utah State University, when Senator Browning visited his family. He enjoyed, and maintains leadership trainings and managerial skills. President of Utah State University Glenn L. Taggart and Dr. Bahman Fakhraie invited Iranian Ambassador Adeshir Zahedi, and world-renowned Iranian entertainers for Nurooz. After earning a Bachelor and a Master's degree at Utah State University, he continued his education at University of Utah. You can study his publications on internet, and at library of congress, as it becomes available, and updated.

$189.95
ISBN 978-0-9852958-3-7
59999>
9 780985 295837

www.ingramcontent.com/pod-product-compliance
Lightning Source LLC
LaVergne TN
LVHW052307200926
848481LV00002B/489